Apostles to the City

Apostles to the City

Biblical Strategies for Urban Missions

Roger S. Greenway

BAKER BOOK HOUSE
Grand Rapids, Michigan

PHOTOLITHOPRINTED BY CUSHING - MALLOY, INC.
ANN ARBOR, MICHIGAN, UNITED STATES OF AMERICA

To my parents,
whose half century of Christian ministry
has enriched many lives in America and
born fruit in remote parts of the earth.

"The voice of the Lord cries to the city."
Micah 6:9 a

Contents

Foreword

Twenty years ago, Roger S. Greenway began his ministry as a missionary to Ceylon (now, Sri Lanka) for the Christian Reformed Church. For five years he and his wife, Edna, worked for the renewal and extension of the Dutch Reformed Church in that island nation, beginning at Colombo.

Fifteen years ago, Rev. Greenway moved to Mexico. He devoted himself ardently to evangelization, church planting, urban outreach, and Bible institute training for national workers. These ministries continued for seven years.

Eight years ago, missionary Greenway turned to postgraduate study at Southwestern Baptist Theological Seminary in Fort Worth, Texas, conducting research in the history and practice of the church's outreach to cities since Bible times. From this study and his own experience in Ceylon and Mexico, Dr. Greenway completed his dissertation and published a book entitled, *Urban Strategy for Latin America*. Subsequently, he was appointed by his denomination as Latin America Secretary for Christian Reformed World Missions.

One year ago, Dr. Greenway presented the annual Baker Mission Lecture series at Reformed Bible College on the theme, "Apostles to the City." In these lectures, the author turned to the Bible for examples and instructions on urban evangelization. The present volume embodies these presentations on Jonah, Jeremiah, Nehemiah, Barnabas, and Paul.

Dr. Greenway's lectures taught and excited students and faculty members alike. They brought biblical history and insights to bear upon conditions facing the church in the world's cities today. We are pleased that Baker Book House is making them available in published form through this volume.

Ten years ago, Reformed Bible College began its annual Mexico Summer Training Session (STS). Dr. and Mrs. Greenway gave much help to that first group and have continued to encourage the development of this missionary orientation course through its first decade. We consider it particularly gratifying that Dr. Greenway has designated all royalties from the sale of this edition for Mexico Summer Training Session and warmly express our thanks to him.

I heartily commend this book to the reader because it speaks so directly to the mission of the church today and because Dr. Greenway is superbly qualified by experience and study to present this material.

Dick L. Van Halsema
President, Reformed Bible College

Introduction

The purpose of this book is to shed light from Scripture on the nature and scope of the church's urban mission. The Bible contains fourteen hundred references to the city, and there are at least twenty-five examples of what can be called urban ministry in the historical books alone. With this amount of scriptural data before us, it is not surprising that both the Old and New Testaments provide examples of outstanding urban ministries which give us important insights into God's will for cities. In the chapters that follow, I will examine a number of these passages and apply their insights to the contemporary world situation. At the same time I have drawn from my own experience in urban mission in Asia and Latin America in the hope that through the interplay of biblical teaching, field experience, and contemporary challenges, new insights will be found that will help us find our way as missionaries in today's cities.

One of the underlying assumptions of this book is that the development of a biblical urban apostolate is vitally needed today. Throughout history God has called his servants to address the gospel to cities, and at no time has this been more urgent than in today's urbanizing world. The twentieth century has witnessed the growth of city populations beyond all expectations. Some cities in Latin America will have twenty million people by the year 2000. In France, one out of every five Frenchmen currently lives in Paris or its satellite communities. The world's largest cities are in Asia, and no one really knows how many people some of these cities contain. North America represents a peculiar situation, with populations flowing both to and from the city and an urban culture which dominates the entire country. The only conclusion we can reach is that at no time in history has it been more true than now that he who wins the city, wins the world. For Christians this makes the development of a biblical and relevant urban apostolate a matter of primary concern.

A second assumption of this book is that the church must move quickly to make its impact on the city, or the city will soon have reshaped the church. If the city shapes the church, we can be sure that the church will no longer be the servant of God with redeeming power for the salvation of men, but will have become a slave to the secular thinking and lifestyles of urban society. In many ways this has happened already, for we see how silent and inert the church can be at those very points in our civilization where decisions are made and actions planned which affect the lives of millions. The church as a whole does not know what to say to the city, and the individual Christian is equally bewildered because the secular spirit has gained so much influence. Therefore, this book also calls for the renewal of the church as a prerequisite for urban apostolate. Without the renewal of the church there is little hope for the city. *— or reality of unity?*

The third assumption is that only a "holistic" approach to urban mission can satisfy either the biblical injunctions or the needs of the city. By holistic mission I mean an approach to the city which first of all proclaims by word and deed the whole Christ, Savior and Lord, Redeemer and King. The church needs the whole gospel—the meaning and implications of the redemptive events of the cross, resurrection, and session at God's right hand must remain together. Second, holistic urban missions refuses to divide human needs into neat segments (such as spiritual, material, psychological), but proclaims the indivisibility of the human person in the redemptive purpose of God. Consequently, holistic mission strategy unites word with deed, worship with service, and fellowship with mission. It takes its cue from what Jesus did and the apostles after him. They came preaching the gospel of the kingdom, which set whole cities in an uproar.

The fourth underlying assumption of this book is expressed in the summary statement of the writer to the Hebrews: "For here we have no lasting city, but we seek the city which is to come" (13:14). The march of the great men of faith throughout the centuries is toward the city. Their pilgrimage, their warfare, their constructive passion, were inspired by the vision of a city—a city well-founded, with order and justice. Its architect and builder is God. If we could write a continuation of Hebrews 11 we would add the names of apostles, martyrs, reformers, statesmen, preachers, and missionaries, who through the years were part of that great march of faith. Seeing the city afar off, they set their faces toward it. They fought fierce battles and suffered severe losses. But they never reached the final goal or saw the city built, for like their predecessors, "all these, though well attested by their faith, did not receive what was promised" (11:39). In our discussions about urban apostolate and the meaning of holistic mission strategy today, we must bear in mind that we are on a pilgrimage of faith and will not see the ultimate accomplished nor the city of God erected here by our efforts. By man's own doing, or even by the vigorous efforts of Christian men and women, cities of earth can never become the city of God which we seek. At the heart of city life, the raw individualism of human selfishness sits enthroned—varying its expression and altering its method with time and place. Consequently, each city bears the seeds of its own destruction. But still the pilgrimage continues, attracting impassioned men who share the dream of the heroes listed in Hebrews, a vision of the city of God, the world at the feet of Jesus—the ultimate goal of urban apostolate.

A major portion of this book was first presented in the form of lectures as part of the Baker Lecture Series at the Reformed Bible College in the spring of 1976. I wish to express my appreciation to Mr. Herman Baker, the sponsor of this series, for his enlightened concern for world mission and his generous support of the lecture series. I am grateful to Dr. Dick Van Halsema and the faculty of the Reformed Bible College of Grand Rapids, Michigan for their invitation to present these lectures. My thanks goes also to Miss Debra Vugteveen, my competent secretary, who patiently typed and retyped the final manuscript in preparation for publication.

Along with principal and practical insights into biblical urban mission, I have sought to weave into every page the sense of urgency I feel for urban evangelization. The cities of the world need modern apostles, men and women of God who have a particular burden for city people. By this I do not imply that rural work is unimportant. But as the world becomes increasingly urban with city populations mushrooming everywhere, we must learn what it means to advance the gospel among city people and plant among them living churches, lighthouses of the kingdom of the Lord Jesus Christ. To that end this book is dedicated.

Roger S. Greenway

Chapter 1

Jonah

Hope for Doomed Cities

The crisis of the cities is worldwide. Almost every major country is wondering what to do with its large cities. In April, 1975, the popular American weekly magazine *U.S. News & World Report* featured a cover story which bore the title, "Cities in Peril."[1] One year later the same magazine featured a sixteen-page special section, again with cover headlines, entitled, "Are *All* Big Cities Doomed?"[2] From "peril" to "doom" in exactly one year is an indication of the worsening condition of large American cities as seen by news analysts who are in close touch with urban life.

Hardly anywhere can you find much sympathy for big cities, at least not among ordinary people who have to live in them. "Cities" and "problems" seem to be synonymous. The city's bewildering diversity, high crime rate, pollution, congestion, poverty, and squalor have created a kind of antiurban prejudice that makes people view cities with undisguised antagonism, and in some cases, self-righteous contempt. Everyone recognizes that cities are the centers of government, the generators of progress, the progenitors of new lifestyles, and the communication centers of the world. Cities are places where new and exciting things happen every day. Yet city lovers are hard to find, and a worldwide antiurban bias is growing everywhere.

---

[1] *U.S. News & World Report,* April 7, 1975.

[2] *Ibid.,* April 5, 1976.

People Problems

The number and complexity of urban problems are directly related to the unrestrained growth of urban populations. Take Mexico City, for example, which was founded in 1325 by the Aztecs. When the Spaniards conquered Mexico in 1512, they kept Mexico City as their capital. After Mexico won its freedom from Spain in 1821, Mexico City became the seat of government for the new republic. Despite this long history, however, Mexico City today is faced with problems that defy solutions.

The scope of these problems is so wide that it touches every aspect of urban life. There is the city's teeming population; inadequate housing; unemployment and underemployment; atmospheric contamination by dust, industrial discharges, and automobile emissions; increasing traffic strangulation; and problems of supplying clean water. When the Spanish discovered Mexico City, it was already one of the world's largest urban settlements, with between three hundred thousand and five hundred thousand inhabitants. But the population of the metropolitan area now numbers over 12 million, and it is predicted that within ten years the population will stand at 18 million people. How can anyone expect urban planners and engineers to supply so many people with adequate housing, safe water, clean air, and decent living?

This same question was asked some time ago by Rubens Vaz da Costa, president of the National Housing Bank of Brazil. He said that today over 60 percent of the Brazilians live in cities and by 1980, two out of every three will be city dwellers. Brazil's cities are growing too fast for the good of the people who live in them. Over 5 million city homes are classified as unfit for human inhabitation. Five hundred thousand units must be built annually just to keep up with the present demand. In 1970 only about 26 percent of Brazil's 54 million urbanites were served by water mains and only 13 million city dwellers had public sewage disposal. There is no way, said Vaz da Costa, that the 80 million who will live in Brazilian cities in 1980 will be able to have the basic public services of clean water, sewage disposal, and electricity.

The problem of providing the basic public services that urban life demands is proving to be insurmountable for many Western cities. The demand for such services has exposed the economic vulnerability of urban centers. New York City nearly went bankrupt in 1975. Throughout the year, arguments raged back and forth between those who insisted that New York bear the responsibility for its own economic situation and not expect the federal government to bail the city out, and those who argued that New York's problems were not exclusively of its own making and the nation as a whole had an obligation to save the country's largest city from financial collapse.

New York's financial crisis became a political issue in the 1976 presidential elections, when all the major candidates were questioned as to their position regarding New York's crisis. The attention was focused on New York because what happened in that city can, and very likely will, happen in other major cities. When millions of people are pressed together—many of them poor, uneducated, and unemployed—the crime rate soars, the quality of education in the schools diminishes, and the demand for public services of all kinds increases. At the same time, when increased tax revenues are needed to meet the demand for public services, taxpayers flee to the suburbs and business organizations relocate. The city is caught in the squeeze. On the one hand taxes rise as more people require welfare assistance, protection, and education; and on the other hand the tax base disappears as people and businesses go elsewhere. Although New York City's problems are larger and more acute than those of most Western cities, they are not unique. The same pressures are felt in every major city of the world, particularly those in which civic administrations try to meet human needs through a variety of social and relief programs.

Many are saying that big cities are doomed, and conditions can only get worse. They point to a host of causes to back up their argument. Cities are becoming dumping grounds for poor people, according to Dr. Pierre de Visé, professor of urban studies at the University of Illinois at Chicago. The moving van has become the symbol of middle-class people's response to the city's deteriorating condition. The belief that the urban situation is hopeless and cities are beyond renewal dampens the initiative of those who still fight for the cities' improvement.

To see how dire social conditions in a city can become, visit Calcutta, the city which Rudyard Kipling described almost a century ago as the "city of dreadful night." Sprawling vast, gray, and smoky along the banks of the swirling Hooghly River, the western-most tributary of the sacred Ganges, Calcutta is so lost in everything big, crowded, and old that its misery defies human description. It is one of the puzzles of history that God has allowed Calcutta to exist for so long. It is estimated that 80 percent of Calcutta's families live in single rooms. This leaves two hundred thousand people for whom the pavement is the only home they know. As many as thirty persons share a single water tap and twenty a single latrine. A fourth of Calcutta's food supply is consumed by rats. Some 40 percent of the students at Calcutta University, which has an enrollment of over one hundred thousand, suffer from malnutrition. Major diseases are endemic. Suffering is beyond description. Calcutta's 8 million people are packed eighty thousand to the square mile—hell on earth, vision of the Apocalypse, and the ultimate in urban degradation in contemporary society. If anyone needs to be motivated to work for urban renewal before doomsday comes, let him visit Calcutta.

The social and economic problems of today's great cities are apparent to everyone. But there is another kind of problem, a bankruptcy of a different sort, which is the central concern of Christians. It is the religious need and spiritual condition of city people. It must be admitted, regrettably, that Christianity has not prospered in modern cities, and Protestantism in particular has found the metropolis an unfavorable environment in which to grow. Cities in Western nations are sprinkled with empty church buildings (for sale at giveaway prices) abandoned by Christians who fled to the suburbs "where decent people live." The Christian missionary enterprise, both home and foreign, has not fared well in big cities, and the reluctance of many missionaries to live and work in big cities has contributed to the city's religious bankruptcy. The antiurban bias that for years has characterized Western Protestant churches is reflected in missionary planning and activity. The problems of the city are so numerous and difficult to solve, and even to live with, that churches have directed their attention elsewhere.

It is my intention in this chapter to speak a word of hope for doomed cities. I shall do so in the context of Jonah's mission to the ancient city of Nineveh, which was a doomed city (Nah. 3:5-7) and yet the object of God's gracious dealings. The evidence of God's concern for Nineveh was seen in the mission which he gave to Jonah, who became the first apostle to the city. Jonah preached to the Ninevites in a bitter and resentful spirit, but despite this God used him. Jonah was a "sign to the men of Nineveh," even as Jesus Christ was a sign to his generation, of God's saving operation (Luke 11:30). The wonder of Nineveh was the manner and extent of the city's repentance, a repentance that prompted Jesus to exclaim:

> The men of Nineveh will arise at the judgment with this generation and condemn it; for they repented at the preaching of Jonah, and behold, something greater than Jonah is here (Luke 11:32, RSV).

There was hope for Nineveh because of God, because of the prophet, and because of the spirit of repentance that swept through the city.

God's Problem with the City

And now!

Had there been urban sociologists in Nineveh's day, they never would have talked about what God saw as the city's fundamental problem. God was grieved by the city's *wickedness*. God made this clear when he commissioned Jonah to go and preach in Nineveh: "Arise," he said, "go to Nineveh, that great city, and cry against it; for their *wickedness* has come up before me" (Jonah 1:2, RSV, italics mine).

Nineveh was a "great city" in many ways. It was a world metropolis and capital of a powerful empire. The city lasted for fifteen hundred years, making most modern cities look like adolescent upstarts by comparison. Nineveh was famous for its beauty, and many considered it the fairest city built on earth since Cain founded Enoch. Militarily, Nineveh seemed impregnable. Its outer ramparts stretched for sixty miles, its inner walls were a hundred feet high. Horse-drawn chariots, three abreast, could ride its battlements. It took ten thousand slaves twelve years to build the king's house, and the city's parks and public buildings were praised throughout the world.

But Nineveh's wealth and opulence invited divine judgment, for they had been gained by oppression, war, and plunder. The entire political and economic life of the city was based on military aggression, the exploitation of weaker nations, and slave labor. The prophet Nahum spared few superlatives in describing this betrayer of nations and city of harlotries (Nah. 3:4). Nineveh was the mistress of witchcrafts and a capital of vice. Her artistic achievements were fouled by obscenities, her culture by idols, and her beauty by violence. She was called "city of blood" (Nah. 3:1), for booty and plunder had made her rich.

Nineveh's wickedness provoked God's wrath. God knew precisely what was going on. He said to Jonah that *"their* wickedness" had come up before him. The sin of the city was personal, for it was committed personally by Nineveh's thousands of inhabitants. It was also collective, for when it was all added up, the sum total of Nineveh's life, culture, and achievements, had *wickedness* written across it. When judgment fell, everyone would be affected. The warp and woof of Ninevitish life was depraved, and the city's only hope consisted in a repentance as wide and complete as the sin that stained it.

Jonah's Reluctance to Save the City

Against the urban monster, one man was called to stand. Jonah, a small town prophet from a third-class nation, was chosen by God to bring the great city to its knees. God's strategy was simple: Jehovah to commission Jonah, Jonah to preach to Nineveh, then Nineveh to return to God. The occasion for the mission was Nineveh's great wickedness and impending doom. The human instrument was a Hebrew prophet. Above all else, divine grace was the motivation. Nineveh was to become a model for urban prophets of all times to consider.

God called Jonah to go to Nineveh, the notoriously wicked capital of the declining Assyrian Empire, and announce God's impending judgment on the city. How long Jonah struggled over the question of whether or not to obey God's commission, the record does not say. But Jonah decided not to go, and instead of going eastward toward Nineveh, he hurried westward to the Mediterranean Sea. At Joppa he boarded a ship with the intention of sailing to Tarshish, away "from the presence of the Lord" (Jonah 1:3).

A storm at sea changed Jonah's plans. The terrified sailors, a mixed crew from many nations, put forth every effort to save themselves and the ship. They rowed hard (Jonah 1:13), and each prayed to his god (Jonah 1:5) while Jonah lay asleep below deck. Roused from sleep by the irate captain and his guilt exposed through the casting of lots, Jonah told all. He identified himself as a Hebrew, one who feared "the Lord, the God of heaven, who made the sea and the dry land" (Jonah 1:9). Hearing this, the mariners nearly panicked, for what they knew about the God of the Hebrews indicated that he was someone to be reckoned with. God's runaway prophet on board was dangerous business (Jonah 1:10), so when all other efforts failed, the sailors did what Jonah suggested: they picked him up and threw him overboard. At once the "sea ceased from raging," and the sailors "feared the Lord exceedingly, and they offered a sacrifice to the Lord and made vows" (Jonah 1:16, RSV).

Now the reluctant prophet was really in trouble. "God has had enough of me," he thought, as down to the bottom he sank. "The waters closed in over me," he said, "weeds were wrapped about my head at the roots of the mountains" (Jonah 2:5, RSV). Jonah figured he was finished, but the unexpected happened. God "appointed a great fish to swallow up Jonah" (Jonah 1:17, RSV) and after three days and three nights in the belly of the fish Jonah came to his senses. Inside the fish, spiritual revival took place. Jonah later recalled:

> "When my soul fainted within me,
> I remembered the Lord;
> and my prayer came to thee,
> into thy holy temple.
> Those who pay regard to vain idols
> forsake their true loyalty.
> But I with the voice of thanksgiving
> will sacrifice to thee;
> what I have vowed I will pay.
> *Deliverance belongs to the Lord!*"
> (Jonah 2:7-9, RSV, italics mine.)

When that note of gratitude and submission came from Jonah, God "spoke to the fish, and it vomited out Jonah upon the dry land" (Jonah 2:10, RSV). Through his own rebellion and God's righteous judgment, Jonah had tasted in a new way God's forbearance and grace. "Salvation, deliverance, is from the Lord," became his personal testimony. Having experienced himself what the city needed to hear, he was prepared for his mission to Nineveh, to be a "sign" to the city of God's mercy as well as his wrath (Luke 11:30).

Commissioned again to go to Nineveh, Jonah turned eastward. Even before he began to preach, he knew in his heart what was likely to happen. As a son of Israel and prophet of God, Jonah knew that God was a "gracious God and merciful, slow to anger, and abounding in steadfast love, and repentest of evil" (Jonah 4:2, RSV). Had not his own nation, Israel, experienced this over and over again? Had not he himself found it to be true in the belly of the fish? When Nineveh repented and God postponed destruction, it came as no surprise to Jonah. He knew what God was like.

When we speak about Jonah's mission to Nineveh, an important point to be observed is this: *the initiative for the entire undertaking comes from God*. It is all a commentary on the prophet's exclamation from the stomach of the fish: "Salvation is from the Lord!" The Book of Jonah begins with a word from God: "Arise, go to Nineveh, that great city, and cry against it; for their wickedness has come up before me" (Jonah 1:2, RSV). God also has the last word in Jonah: "And should not I pity Nineveh, that great city, in which there are more than a hundred and twenty thousand persons who do not know their right hand from their left, and also much cattle?" (Jonah 4:11, RSV). Between these verses lies a narrative in which the leading human actor is Jonah, but the principal, divine actor is God. It is a story about Jonah, yet the initiative is always God's. God forces the issue at every turn. God threatens judgment on Nineveh; he sends the prophet to preach in Nineveh's streets; he stops Jonah's flight by a storm and saves him by a fish; he spares the repentant city, as an act of his pity and grace: he provides the gourd; he "appoints" the worm; he sends the sultry east wind; and he rebukes the prophet. The Book of Jonah is a stirring account of God in action on behalf of a wicked city. Properly speaking, it is God's mission before it is Jonah's. *But he didn't send an economist/not a social worker - not a conservative, militarist Republican - he sent a prophet - seeking repentance.*

The City's Repentance

Nineveh's phenomenal response to Jonah's preaching pleased God and forestalled the city's destruction. The entire population repented. The Bible does not tell us the entire content of Jonah's message, but it does make clear that God told Jonah to preach judgment: "Yet forty days, and Nineveh shall be overthrown"

(Jonah 3:4, RSV). Jonah minced no words. No "easy invitation" was given. Judgment and destruction were imminent, and the most gracious act Jonah could do was to tell the Ninevites what to expect. The result was a miracle: "And the people of Nineveh believed God; they proclaimed a fast, and put on sackcloth, from the greatest of them to the least of them" (Jonah 3:5 RSV).

Nineveh's radical response to Jonah's preaching began with the common people and spread to the palace (Jonah 3:6). Upon hearing the news of what was happening in the streets, the king of Nineveh arose from his throne, removed his royal robe, covered himself with sackcloth and sat in ashes (Jonah 3:6). What an unlikely response from a threatened monarch! No retaliation against the foreign apostle who had aroused the peoples' sense of guilt; no royal order to get back to work and forget this religious nonsense; no repression of the public demonstration of national shame and repentance. Instead, the king made a proclamation and published it throughout the city:

> "By the decree of the king and his nobles: Let neither man nor beast, herd nor flock, taste anything; let them not feed, or drink water, but let man and beast be covered with sackcloth, and let them cry mightily to God; yea, let everyone turn from his evil way and from the violence which is in his hands. Who knows, God may yet repent and turn from his fierce anger, so that we perish not?" (Jonah 3:7-9, RSV).

The king accepted God's judgment as just, and he made no attempt to bargain his way out. He called for a city-wide, unconditional act of repentance. As the political head of the city, and probably its religious head too, he bowed before the judgment of God. He hoped that God might yet show mercy, but the demonstration of repentance which he called was no sham nor an attempt to manipulate God. The prophet had said the city was doomed, and the king believed it. Like Jonah in the fish, the king and his people could only cry to God and hope for mercy.

Just as Nineveh's solidarity in sin precipitated God's judgment, the city's solidarity in repentance was the clue to its pardon. God forgave when king and commoner, rich and poor, and labor and management together joined in public contrition and personal conversion from their evil ways and from the violence which they had perpetrated against their neighbors. As a sign of the city's solidarity in repentance even the *animals* were made to fast (Jonah 3:7,8). As animals they were incapable of making moral decisions, of "sinning" in the sense of acting responsibly in matters of moral conduct. But animals were vital to the city's life. The city could not work or move without them, and to underscore the city's solidarity in repentance the animals were included in the public fasting. Their thirsty moans blended with the peoples' prayers in repentance toward God. It comes as no surprise, therefore, that Nineveh's animals are mentioned again at the close of the book where God speaks of his pity toward the city (Jonah 4:11).

The solidarity of society in sin is not easy for twentieth-century people to recognize, for the concept of social sin sounds foreign to our ears. Schooled as we are in the view that sin is exclusively an individual matter, and similarly that repentance can only happen on a one-by-one basis, the repentance of Nineveh seems almost incomprehensible. At Nineveh, an entire urban populace recognized the fact that wickedness had become a way of life, and God's judgment on their society was justified. They did not argue with the prophet or deny the justice of the doom he foretold. There was no appeal to some "higher court." The repentance of the Ninevites was both personal and corporate. Each living being had to put off evil, fast, pray to God, and wear clothing of repentance. Certain individuals and segments of society were undoubtedly more guilty than others, but that was not the issue. They were all in it together—in sin and in judgment. So also, in repentance. It was their *manner* of repentance, as much as the *fact* that the city repented, that made Nineveh a model for all cities and their inhabitants.

Lessons from Jonah for Modern Urban Mission

Many lessons can be drawn from the Jonah story. The first concerns our understanding of God himself. Holy God is very concerned about unholy people. Nineveh was a wicked city, infamous the world over for its bloody wars of plunder and oppression of helpless people. It was a heathen city in every respect, full of idolatry and vice. Yet the holy God of Israel wanted his servant, Jonah, to get involved with that city. He sent him to its streets to preach a message that would result in repentance and a postponement of divine judgment. The God who loved Israel was also concerned about Nineveh, and he found no pleasure in seeing the Ninevites destroyed.

Religious Israel did not conceive of God in these terms. Consequently, Jonah had a theological problem when God sent him to Nineveh, and the conflict between Jonah's way of thinking about God and the clear implications of his assignment was irreconcilable. For God was revealing himself in terms of universal concern and with a forbearance toward the nations beyond Israel that Jonah and his coreligionists found difficult to accept.

The church, God's new Israel, has a similar problem. It is constantly tempted to be concerned exclusively with itself and ignore the unsaved world outside. Pastors minister faithfully to the flock but find it difficult to break away in search of lost and straying sheep. Theologians develop dogma but neglect missions. Evangelism gets only a small percentage of church budgets. The historic Christian creeds include many great statements about God and his work. But where, except by implication, do they set forth the missionary nature of God and the missionary character of the church? Internal affairs are the principal concerns of Israel, new and old, and insofar as this attitude prevails the Jonah syndrome continues. God sees Nineveh, but his people do not. And because they do not, they really do not understand him.

Second, we can draw a lesson concering the prophetic vocation. As a man called of God, Jonah represented all who have heard God's call to serve him in faraway places and found it very difficult to carry out their mission. As far as we know, Jonah was faithful to his calling as a prophet as long as he was allowed to stay within the borders of Israel. In Israel he was bold, and he even told the king what God wanted him to do (II Kings 14:25). But when God called him to Nineveh, the great and wicked foreign city, Jonah's courage failed, his calling as God's prophet grew dim, and he fled in the opposite direction. In this sense, Jonah represents all reluctant and runaway prophets who have heard God's call, but "went down to Joppa," and did something else.

Third, Jonah represented Israel, the people of God elected from among the nations to be objects and channels of his grace, his witnesses among the peoples. In the words of Isaiah 43:10-12,

Israel was to be a nation of witnesses to the uniqueness of God and his salvation:

"You are my witnesses," says the Lord,
"and my servant whom I have chosen,
that you may know and believe me
and understand that I am He.
Before me no god was formed,
nor shall there be any after me.
I, I am the Lord,
and besides me there is no savior.
I declared and saved and proclaimed,
when there was no strange god among you;
and you are my witnesses," says the Lord (RSV).

Israel had forgotten the nation's calling to be witnesses of God's deliverance before the nations. Divine election had come to be viewed as Israel's election to privilege, not to service and witness. Israel's people viewed the nations as means by which God periodically chastened his chosen people, but never as objects of divine grace and concern. The world existed for Israel, not Israel for the world. People like the Ninevites were born to be burned, not to be preached into repentance and saved. Therefore, to the Hebrew mind, God's command to preach to Nineveh was incongruous and incomprehensible. But for a few perceptive souls the message sank in, and they caught the point of God's rebuke. God was concerned about the wicked city. There was saving mercy in God's heart for the nations beyond Israel. And there was a role for Israel to play which God would not let her forget.

Fourth, a lesson can be drawn from the Jonah narrative concerning the strategy of missions. Just as Nineveh, as the capital of ancient Assyria, was the logical place for an effort aimed at influencing the entire nation, so the great cities of our day are the strategic centers that must be won if nations are to be discipled. Failure in winning the cities means failure in discipling the world. This being the case, we must ask why it is that in today's situation such an overwhelming proportion of missionary resources goes toward evangelizing out-of-the-way places, mountain hamlets, and jungle recesses, while great cities are relatively neglected. Is there a lesson in Jonah which we continue to ignore? Cities are the places where the destinies of nations are determined. Cities are the centers of communication, commerce, cul-

26

tural life, and government. As the cities go, so go the nations. If winning the nations to Christ is our assignment, to the cities we must go. Yet, sadly we must confess that many of God's servants are in the same position as Jonah on the hillside, watching the city from a safe distance and caring little whether it lives or dies.

Finally, God speaks through Jonah about the nature of urban mission. So much of what is called "urban mission" never gets to the reason why God sent Jonah to Nineveh in the first place, namely, the *wickedness* of the city. There are two serious weaknesses in most of the so-called urban mission work done in cities. First, there is an almost exclusive preoccupation with the *results* of sin, that is, the human misery that sin produces. And second, there is widespread ignorance of and indifference to the *breadth and depth* of urban sin.

It is tragic that Marxist writers describe more profoundly than most Christian writers the manner in which wickedness operates in the city. The writings of Marxists rather than Christian preaching more clearly describe and condemn the way in which the mishandling of money and power, lust, and racial prejudice are dooming Western societies. Why is this? How is it that middle-class Christianity has allowed itself to settle for a watered-down, comfortable notion of sin, while non-Christian writers are plummeting the depths of society's wickedness? Social wickedness for most middle-class Christians has been reduced to those outward signs of antisocial behavior which shake or threaten middle-class people. But the more subtle types of sin—the deep-seated racism; the corporate violence of a society manipulated by the rich and powerful, enslaving and oppressing whole segments of the human family—are blithefully ignored. In view of this, it is no wonder that our "success" in evangelism is only in terms of individual converts, who are often the "marginal" people of society, whereas the great Ninevehs of our day continue in their wickedness, unchallenged by God's prophets.

To all these things, Jonah speaks. With Nineveh, God's struggle to save cities began. Because of Nineveh, there is still hope for cities. Urban mission work began in Nineveh, and in a sense, it must still begin there.

Jeremiah

How to Be a City Saint

In January of 1962, I delivered an address at the annual Christian School Teachers Conference in the Asian city of Colombo, Ceylon (Sri Lanka). The atmosphere in the country was tense and uncertain. Bewilderment marked the teachers' faces, for the Buddhist-dominated government had unexpectedly taken over all the church and mission-owned schools. Many teachers feared for their jobs, and nearly everyone was sure that this would be the last time such a conference could be held. The era of the Christian day schools appeared to be ended, and the role of the church in education seemed to be over.

What appropriate words could be used for such an occasion? The hearts of men and women were heavy. The takeover of the Christian schools was not the only cause for alarm in this tiny nation, for the society as a whole seemed to be going in the wrong direction. Christians in all areas of life were being discriminated against, and a movement was afoot to make Sunday a work day. Any Christian that opposed the trend risked losing his job, resulting in suffering for his family. Many had already decided to emigrate. They felt that the country had become a modern Babylon—violent, unjust, and pagan.

After much consideration, I selected the passage of Psalm 137:1-4, emphasizing the fourth verse.

> By the waters of Babylon,
>   there we sat down and wept,
> when we remembered Zion.
> On the willows there

we hung up our lyres.
For there our captors
required of us songs,
and our tormentors, mirth, saying,
"Sing us one of the songs of Zion!"
How shall we sing the Lord's song
in a foreign land? (RSV, italics mine).

The men and women who were present felt very much like the Hebrew prisoners in ancient Babylon. They were caught in a political, moral, and religious situation which they feared and disliked intensely. They longed for the old social order when, under British colonial rule, Christianity was the favored religion and Christian institutions enjoyed freedom and opportunity. These Christian teachers were tempted to give up, to "hang their harps on the willows," and regard the situation as hopeless. "How," they were asking in effect, "can we sing the Lord's song in a situation like this?"

The message was simple—regardless of the circumstances, the Lord's song must be sung! That was Jeremiah's message to the captive Hebrews in Babylon, and it was relevant in this situation. Because of their sin, God had allowed Israel to be captured and taken to a hostile, foreign city. But Israel's unique character as the people of God had not been removed, nor had Israel's mission among the nations been terminated. Babylon was a wicked and idolatrous city, ultimately doomed to be destroyed. Yet it was precisely in that situation that Israel was required to fulfill its calling as a holy people, set apart from among the nations to be witnesses of the one true God (Deut. 14:1, 2; Isa. 43:10). Israel in Babylon was still a people with a mission, and that mission was God-defined:

> "Thus says the Lord of hosts, the God of Israel, to all the exiles whom I have sent into exile from Jerusalem to Babylon: Build houses and live in them; plant gardens and eat their produce. Take wives and have sons and daughters in marriage, that they may bear sons and daughters; multiply there, and do not decrease. But seek the welfare of the city where I have sent you into exile, and pray to the Lord on its behalf, for in its welfare you will find your welfare" (Jer. 29:4-7, RSV).

The people were not to escape the city or sit in sullen rebellion. Though the city was wicked, they must not seek to destroy it.

They must build houses, plant gardens, marry, and beget children. Their population was to increase, not decrease. Their role was to be salvatory, not destructive. As God's people they were to seek in every way the city's welfare, its shalom in the fullest sense. Prayer to Jehovah on behalf of the city was to be the most profound expression of the people's attitude. In the welfare of Babylon, Israel would find its own well-being.

A Formula for City Saints

God's word to Israel in Babylon provides us with a formula for city saints. It tells us how God wants his people to live and witness in the city. That was the issue facing the Hebrews in Babylon, and it is the question faced by city Christians today. Like the ancient Hebrews, many Christians ignore their mission, which to a great extent explains why city churches are so weak and cities are so bad. But the Scriptures are plain enough, and both the Old and New Testaments present the same message.

Writing to first-century Christians, most of whom lived in cities, Peter said: "You are a chosen race, a royal priesthood, a holy nation, God's own people, that you may declare the wonderful deeds of him who called you out of darkness into his marvelous light" (I Peter 2:9, RSV). To "declare the wonderful deeds of God" was another way of saying, "Sing the Lord's song." Christians scattered here and there in Graeco-Roman cities were regarded as "aliens and exiles"; they were accused of being traitors and tempted to abandon the faith (I Peter 2:11, 12). But there was to be no "hanging of the harps in the willows." Christians had a life to live and a message to proclaim. In short, they were called to be apostles to the city.

Presence in the City

God's word to Israel in Babylon was, "Build houses . . . plant gardens." In other words, consider the city where I have placed you to be your home and stay there.

For the Hebrews in Babylon, it was not a question of whether or not they could choose to remain in the city. They were captives, and if liberation came at all, it would be by an act of God (Jer. 29:14). The challenges facing Israel were these: Would they repent from the sinful ways that had precipitated the exile? Would they keep the faith despite pagan surroundings and the false prophets and prophetesses in their midst (Jer. 29:8, 9)? Would they fulfill their mandate as God's special people, his witnesses to the nations and now especially to Babylon? In other words, would Israel be renewed during the exile and once again carry out its redemptive role on earth?

For many Christians today, presence in the city is a matter of choice,—a religious decision. To live in "Babylon" by choice requires a special sense of calling. Residence in the city often involes a certain amount of risk, and possibly sacrifice. Increasingly it means overcoming racial barriers and living among people of another culture, moral standard, and ethnic identity. To the extent in which individuals, families, and churches are convinced that urban presence is God's will for them, they will accept the challenge to remain in the city and bear witness there. Without the conviction that it is God's will to maintain Christian presence in the city, urban residence is hardly worth the price, nor is it likely to have any salvatory effect.

On the American scene today, a major shift in population is occurring. It is a movement away from the big cities. Where once Americans thronged to the cities and their immediate suburbs in search of jobs, education, and excitement, today they are moving in the opposite direction, toward the smaller towns and more distant suburbs. Between 1970 and 1974, 1.7 million more Americans left the big metropolitan areas than moved to them. Through migration, the New York area alone lost half a million people. Of the sixteen metropolitan areas in America that have more than 2 million people each, eight have lost population since 1970. Partly as a cause and partly as an effect of this migration, the quality of life in American cities is declining, problems are multiplying, and the human leadership needed to reverse the trend is becoming more difficult to find.

The reasons for the exodus are not hard to determine: urban crime, pollution, over-crowded schools, noise, high taxes, the high cost of living in general, and the impersonality of the city. Racial aversion is behind the flight of many whites, although, blacks, too, have joined the movement away from the city. Nevertheless, the danger is increasing that America may develop into a kind of *apartheid* society, with the blacks concentrated in the cities and the whites in the suburbs and small towns.

What is the Christian response to the question of continued residence in the city? To non-Christians, the only question to be asked is the pragmatic one: Where is the most pleasant and convenient place to live, work, and raise a family? But for Christians there are other things to consider. Christians are not their own, but they belong to God, and the Lord has assignments for all his servants. The question of where one selects a home and establishes residence is a religious question. It is to be decided through prayer and as an act of faith. It must not only be compatible with, but a result of one's understanding of God's will for his life and the task God expects him to carry out in society.

In view of God's continued concern for cities, any Christian contemplating flight to the suburbs should give the most careful consideration to what he is doing. The Scriptures reveal that at every key turning point in redemptive history, God sends his servants to the city to proclaim his word and herald his kingdom. The closing decades of the twentieth century are, by all estimates, one of history's greatest hours. God wants his witnesses in the key centers of culture, commerce, politics, and communication, and without exception these centers are the great cities. What irony, what tragedy it is that while God can be seen moving *toward* the city, God's people move in the opposite direction. This cannot be understood in any other way than as an abandonment of the task God calls Christians to perform and a denial of the mission received from the Lord.

strong!

"Multiply, Do Not Decrease"

In Jeremiah's instructions to the Hebrews in Babylon, acceptance of the city as the place where God wanted them to be was related to the begetting of children (Jer. 29:6). The willingness to marry, give their children in marriage, and beget children and multiply, connoted acceptance of the city and adjustment to it. In the contemporary world, rejection of the city as a suitable place for life and progeny is seen in the return of Third World mothers to the villages from which they came when the time approaches for a child to be born. Despite the fact that the city offers them modern medical facilities, some women prefer going back to their villages where they must give birth on a hard dirt floor, attended only by semitrained midwives. By so doing, they say in effect that the city is not their home and they do not care to bear

33

children in the urban environment. On the other hand, acceptance of the city is indicated when a woman decides to stay in the city to bear her children. Once she has made that decision, her adjustment to the city is rapid and she no longer regards herself as essentially a peasant living in the city.

At a time when the birthrate in the United States and in other traditionally Christian countries has dropped to its lowest point in history, the divine injunction to Israel, "multiply . . . and do not decrease" (Jer. 29:6), raises some interesting questions. Is zero pupulation growth a justifiable goal from the Christian standpoint? Urban experts point to the city's over-crowded housing, unemployment, crime, and spiralling cost of welfare services, and they tell us that if urban civilization is to survive there must be a decrease in the rate of human fertility. The majority of Americans seem to agree with this opinion, for recent polls indicate that an increasing number of couples either want no children or fewer children than their parents had.

Although to increase and multiply is an unpopular idea in many circles today, the Christian cannot accept the majority opinion uncritically. There are religious dimensions to the subject which secular analysts ignore. The predicaments of modern society are not simply due to the fact that there seem to be more people than the earth can support. Basically, the problems of society are caused by sin and by the unwise and unjust ways people have handled the world's resources. Simply reducing the number of people may relieve some of the pressure, but it does nothing to solve the real problem. Christians should resist the temptation to accept without question the opinions expressed by secular writers, for vital religious considerations are almost always left out of secular analyses of the causes of urban problems and suggested solutions.

Seeking the Shalom of the City

"But seek the welfare [shalom] of the city," said God through Jeremiah to the Hebrews in Babylon, and that was the most important and comprehensive assignment they could be given. Not counting the various proper names such as Salem, Jerusalem, Absalom, and Solomon, there are more than three hundred fifty places in the Old Testament in which shalom or its derivatives appear. The root meaning of shalom is to be whole, sound, saved. Fundamental to the idea of shalom is totality. The fulness of life is involved. Anything that contributes to this wholeness makes for shalom, and anything that stands in the way disrupts shalom. God is the source and foundation of shalom, and in the last analysis there is no shalom apart from him.

In the New Testament, shalom is most often translated "peace" (*eirēnē*), though no single word, either in Greek or in English, can adequately express its meaning. Everything the Old Testament teaches about shalom provides background and understanding to this great concept. Peace is vertical and horizontal. It stands for right relationship with God and right relationships on earth among people who are learning to walk in step with one another. It means peace with God through the person and work of Christ, the Prince of Peace, and peace among men who live by the Spirit and do God's will. It is the life of the kingdom and an ongoing enterprise. The mission of the church is to live peace and proclaim it, doing both within the context of a world that is out of step with God and out of step with itself.

In modern cities shalom is attacked and undermined in a thousand ways, and therein lies the root of urban problems. The mission of the church is to proclaim, promote, and demonstrate shalom amid all the hindrances which sin throws against it. The urban apostolate of the people of God is to be agents of shalom in the midst of the city. To carry out this mission they must understand the following implications of the shalom they are called to establish.

1. *Shalom creates community.* Loneliness, which results from the lack of community, is an indication that life in the city is failing. Where shalom exists, each individual is important, each person plays a part, and each one knows that there is meaning and purpose to his life. The warmth of community relationship dispels the cold loneliness of insignificance.

But what is the situation in modern cities? In Brazil, which expects to add around 30 million people to its already crowded cities in the next ten years, there is a new organization called "Neurotics Anonymous." It is patterned after the well-known Alcoholics Anonymous. Neurotics Anonymous is designed to meet the needs of lonely city people, people who have no one to talk to, no one to whom they can go when their problems become unbearable. Neurotics Anonymous offers lonely people an opportunity to talk to someone on the telephone and meet with others once a week. The members of Neurotics Anonymous cling to each other because no one else seems to care about them as individuals.

Here is an area about which Christians ought to be deeply concerned. Is not *koinonia*, ("fellowship"), one of the church's chief characteristics?

2. *Shalom in the city means concern about the material and physical prosperity of its citizens.* The presence of poverty, slum housing, and unemployment is evidence that life has gone wrong in the city, and shalom has been violated. Oftentimes Christians fail to realize that God expects them to be concerned about poverty, suffering, and injustice, and they raise the bogey of the "social gospel" to warn Christians away from secular involvements. But such neglect of the "horizontal" dimensions of life in favor of exclusive concern with the "vertical" is not biblical Christianity at all. God's mandate is to seek the shalom of the city, and that includes the physical and material well-being of its citizens.

3. *Shalom means trust, confidence, and mutual concern between neighbors.* Where there is deceit and treachery, concern only for one's self and family without concern for neighbors and fellow citizens, shalom is violated and community life disrupted. This points up the fact that in almost every place in the Old Testament where shalom appears, the emphasis falls on the interpersonal nature of human life. Shalom is found where people live in a right relationship with one another. There is trust, confidence, and mutual concern. The New Testament describes the shalom-life in terms of the life of love. It is loving your neighbor as you love yourself.

The Israelites in Babylon had much to ponder when they heard Jeremiah's instruction to "seek the shalom of the city." For they were the people with whom God had established the covenant of shalom, and the shalom-life was the essence of their national character. At every level—family, tribe, city, and nation—Israel was to live out the implications of shalom, and its influence was meant to permeate all areas of Hebrew life.

In Babylon the people were told to seek the shalom of the community beyond the ethnic borders of Israel. This added a new dimension to Israel's religious understanding, and it required a radical reorientation of the people's pattern of thinking. The situation in Babylon was discouraging. In the "old days," back in Palestine, the theocracy had provided a social and political context favorable to the exercise of true religion. National religious life fluctuated, to be sure, and there were many long periods of widespread idolatry and sin. But still, the temple was there, the religious ceremonies that Moses had prescribed were carried on, and there was always a true prophet around somewhere to speak God's Word and teach the people righteousness.

But in Babylon? Here the people of the covenant were thrown into a pagan, hostile, and racially mixed environment. Could God expect them to seek the shalom of this uncircumcised crowd? Could Israel be required to identify with a city such as Babylon and build a relationship of trust and mutual concern with this people? The concept was revolutionary, and it beckoned Israel to understand divine mission in a way which was hard to accept. Yet that was precisely what the prophet said: "Seek the shalom of the city." Even if that city is Babylon.

4. *Shalom has reference to righteousness, in the sense of "just" and "fair" relationship between people.* Without righteousness there cannot be shalom (Isa. 32:16-18; 48:17-19; 60:15-22). There is no shalom to the wicked, nor can an unrighteous society expect to enjoy shalom's benefits (Isa. 48:22; 57:21; 59:8). Bribery, corruption, dishonesty, and cheating destroy shalom and undermine society's welfare. The righteousness in society to which shalom refers is not defined by public opinion or the mores of a given community, but by divinely established standards of right and wrong, of truth and falsehood. Nor is righteousness the same as what is legal, for there are immoral acts which human courts declare legal. God is the fountain of righteousness, and he is its final judge. Human laws and customs and the structures which govern society must conform to God's standards if that society is to enjoy divine blessing and truly promote the well-being of its citizens.

5. *Shalom, above all else, means peace with God and reconciliation with the Maker and Ruler of the universe.* Shalom, you see, means right relationships both vertically (with God) and horizontally (with our fellow man). Old Testament and New Testament revelations blend together to provide the full, rich message of shalom. The essence of the gospel may be expressed in one word, shalom. "You know the word which he [God] sent to Israel,"

said Peter to Cornelius, "preaching good news of *peace* by Jesus Christ (he is Lord of all)" (Acts 10:36, RSV, italics mine). To the Ephesians, Paul wrote: ". . . shod your feet with the equipment of the gospel of *peace*" (Eph. 6:15, RSV, italics mine). All the New Testament teachings about reconciliation, redemption, forgiveness, adoption, and justification are built upon and included in the concept of shalom. Jesus Christ, the Prince of Peace, is the source and mediator of shalom. Through him, shalom comes to earth and joy is restored to human life (Luke 2:10, 14). For this reason, shalom in the Old Testament always has a messianic tone, for it points forward to the coming of the one who alone can remove the barriers between God and man and between man and man, and establish a kingdom in which truth, love, righteousness, and joy prevail.

Shalom has cosmic and eschatological dimensions. Just as the earth and the universe came under the curse because of man's sin, they shall share in the peace of the sons of God. "The creation," writes Paul, "waits with eager longing for the revealing of the sons of God; for the creation was subjected to futility, not of its own will but by the will of him who subjected it in hope; because the creation itself will be set free from its bondage to decay and obtain the glorious liberty of the children of God" (Rom. 8:19-21, RSV). Because of this, Israel's mandate to seek the shalom of the city extended to the natural as well as the spiritual order, to animal life as well as human life, to the welfare of the trees and rivers of Babylon as well as the health and preservation of human life. Shalom has implications for everything that is city.

Incarnation and Proclamation

God's people in Babylon were instructed to identify with the city, for in the shalom of the city they would find their own shalom (Jer. 29:7). They were called to be a people set apart, but the quality of their separation had to shine forth in the context of identification. Like the Prince of shalom who someday would come incarnate, they were to be in the world, but not of it; share its burdens, but not its sins. The Israelites were to give themselves for the welfare of the city, for in the prosperity and peace of Babylon they would find their own satisfaction and security.

As agents of God's shalom, Israel could not be quiet in Babylon. They had a message to tell as well as a distinctive life to live.

Actions alone were not enough. Shalom had to be acted out and also spoken out. God's people had a divine word to communicate, and their mission to Babylon could not be fulfilled without God's revelation being spoken to the city.

This raises an interesting question, for if there was ever a time when silence might have been justified it was the time of Israel's captivity in Babylon. Was Israel in any fit condition to speak redemptively and prophetically to Babylon? Did their prophets really have a word from the Lord from which Babylon might benefit? Or was this a time when Israel ought to remain silent, reflect upon their own moral condition, and wait for the Lord to heal their wounds? The spiritual condition of Israel at that time was horrendous, and that very condition had precipitated the exile. Was Israel in a proper condition to communicate shalom's message to Babylon?

To be sure, the necessity of oral proclamation does not mean that God's people need to be talking all the time. There are times when silence is necessary. Sometimes, unfortunately, the church has spoken when it ought to have remained silent, just as it has often remained silent when it ought to have spoken.

There are circumstances in which believers should not even attempt to speak; situations in which the church has become so confused, so uncertain about its message, or has identified itself so completely with a secular culture that it is in danger of declaring untruth in the name of God. There may be instances when spokesmen for the church have succumbed to outside and anti-Christian forces with the result that their pronouncements result in death instead of life. In such circumstances the church should remain silent, and Christians can only pray for the spirit of repentance and for new and better days.

In such circumstances, actions are also quite useless. For where the spiritual climate has dipped so low that Christians do not know their message and dare not attempt to communicate it, neither their speech nor actions can have any salvatory effect.

Though at times silence is necessary, the verbal proclamation of God's Word remains the continuing mission of his people, and the responsibility to communicate in this fashion rested with Israel in Babylon as well. There was no other way for the full impact of shalom to be felt. Verbal proclamation was, then as now, a dangerous business, and Israel was tempted to avoid the risk of harassment and persecution by remaining silent. But new things do not happen as a result of timidity, and if Israel was to be the Lord's witness in Babylon, shalom had to be spoken as well as lived with all its implications.

Prayer for the City

Jeremiah's instruction to the exiles in Babylon included a word about prayer. "But seek the welfare of the city where I have sent you into exile, *and pray to the Lord on its behalf* . . ." (Jer. 29:7, RSV, italics mine).

In Genesis 18, we read that Abraham interceded for the wicked city of Sodom (Gen. 18:22-33). Six times he asked God to spare Sodom, and each time God granted his petition. Sodom was frightfully wicked, so wicked in fact that there were not even ten righteous people to be found within its gates. Yet for the sake of just ten, God would have saved the city. What was the significance of this handful of righteous people in such a sinful environment? They were agents of shalom, a righteous leaven in an unrighteous loaf. The city could go on only as long as it contained these bearers of God's Word. Without them the city was doomed.

Prayer for the city is a holy war against all the hostile forces that militate against the peace and well-being of the city. By their prayer, God's people distinguish themselves from those who delight in evil. Like priests, they intercede that the city be spared, that its good be promoted, that its sins be forgiven, and that all citizens come to know the fulness of shalom.

Prayer for the city is missionary prayer. It pleads that Christ's lordship be established in the city. One of the reasons there are secular cities in nations that have known the gospel for many years is that our prayers and our witness have been meager and narrow. We have not prayed as we ought that the shalom of Jesus Christ penetrate the corridors of government, the courts of justice, the circles of commerce and business, and the great educational institutions of the land. Because we have not prayed, we have not made an impact for Christ in countless areas of urban life.

Much more needs to be said to help Christians translate words and theory into apostolic purpose and concrete decisions. For Christians who accept the challenge to be "city saints," agents of shalom in metropolis, these are some suggestions:

1. *Live in the city by choice.* If you are now located in a suburb, consider moving back into the city to be a light and witness for Christ. If this is impossible, give personal and moral support to those individuals, families, and churches that want to stay in or move back to the city.

2. *Support programs that are designed to help inner-city people.* In every city there are church-related and community programs that need funds and volunteer help to assist individuals and families that have problems which they cannot solve by themselves. Learn what it means to "go the second mile" with an inner-city family, whether that mile is material, physical, or spiritual.

3. *Get involved in denominational or interdenominational city mission work.* Find out what is going on, offer to help, and give as much input as you can on the basis of your understanding of what urban apostolate involves.

4. *Become acquainted with inner-city people of a minority race.* If they need help, render it yourself or assist them in finding an agency which can meet their need. Oftentimes, inner-city families are not aware of the social services that are available, or they need help in taking advantage of these services.

5. *Encourage open housing.* Through your neighborhood association or other circles of influence, do what you can to make sure that whites are shown houses in racially mixed areas as well as in all-white neighborhoods, and that blacks are shown homes in all-white areas as well as in racially mixed districts. Also insist on equitable mortgage loans for all races and for all parts of the city.

6. *Urge your church to show Christian concern for inner-city people.* If your church is located in the city, urge the evangelism committee to try innovative reach-out programs that will combine both word and deed in the name of Christ and will reach all races and social classes within a certain radius of the church building. If yours is a suburban church, urge the church to join in a partnership relation with an inner-city church to help them minister in the city.

7. *Support adult education, literacy programs, and social services offered by the community.* Through every avenue open to you encourage all good endeavors to help the poor and promote a better life for all citizens. At the same time, actively oppose every

enterprise or influence that you feel is damaging to the social and moral health of the city and its inhabitants.

8. *Pray for the city*. Pray big prayers, prayers that cover the full range of urban life, the poor, the power centers, the communications media, the commercial and industrial worlds, and the political leaders. Pray for city churches and the Christians who comprise them, that they will not abandon their urban mission but will be true agents of shalom in the city.

Chapter 3

Nehemiah

The Secret of Urban Renewal

On December 23, 1972, the Central American capital city of Managua, Nicaragua, was devastated by a terrible earthquake. At twenty-five minutes past midnight, three awesome tremors struck the city. The first two sent vertical vibrations through the buildings, tearing everything loose. The third tremor seemed to move in a horizontal direction, knocking down buildings like a giant bowling ball. Within three minutes, a city of four hundred thousand inhabitants was destroyed.

The president of the Nicaraguan Red Cross, George Cardenas, gave this account of what took place during the days immediately following the devastating earthquake: "The Red Cross used bulldozers to dig one large, common grave which would hold several thousand bodies. People pulled their dead loved ones from the rubble and carried their bodies to the grave site on doors taken from the ruins. They deposited the doors along with the bodies in the common grave."

Precisely how many people were killed on that night of terror no one knows. The Red Cross estimates that between six thousand and eight thousand died, with an additional forty thousand injured. Some people simply disappeared and no one knows what became of them. Parents searched in vain for children who may have been rescued and taken to orphanages, in some cases in foreign countries where they would never be heard from again.

For the residents of Managua, the night of the earthquake was a taste of doomsday, and the spiritual needs of many hearts were brought to light. Managuans had never been known for their interest in religion. A large Roman Catholic cathedral stood in the center of the city, but the vast majority of the population seldom attended its services. Protestant churches were scattered throughout the municipal area, but most Managuans ignored them. On the night of the earthquake, the downtown area, which was the hardest hit by the tremors, was crowded with party-goers. Restaurants and nightclubs were filled, for it was the height of the Christmas season. Managuans were in a festive mood, and very few had any thoughts about God.

But the earthquake changed all that. When the first quake hit the city, the largest downtown Protestant church was severely damaged but remained standing. Huge cracks ran up and down its stately walls and it seemed that at any moment the roof would collapse. Still it remained standing, and hundreds of people tried to press through its doors. Church officials did their best to keep the people out, for they feared what might happen should another tremor strike. At last they succeeded in shutting the doors, and the pastor pleaded with the terrified people in the street not to attempt to push the doors open. But hundreds insisted that if they had to die they wanted to die in a church, even a Protestant church. The building, they reasoned, stood for God and the way to heaven, and they wanted desperately to get in. From the crowded entrance came the cry, *"Déjanos entrar, déjanos entrar"* ("Let us in, let us in").

One of the most moving scenes on that terrible night was that of people kneeling in the streets praying to God as they had never prayed before. Their homes were gone, their possessions lost, and some of their loved ones trapped beneath the rubble. Many thought that the end of the world had come, and in a city in which 95 percent of the population had had no connection with gospel-preaching churches and only a few had shown an interest in religion at all, more praying took place that night than the city had ever seen before.

Relief agencies, both secular and religious, responded to the Managua tragedy. Money, medicine, and food poured into the city. Temporary living quarters were erected, tons of food distributed, and the rebuilding of an entire metropolitan area undertaken. The renewal and rebuilding of the city continues to this day, and it will be years before all the effects of the earthquake are gone. Thousands of Managuans will carry to their graves the scars, both physical and mental, which resulted from that terrible night.

Beyond offering material relief, food for the starving, blankets for the shivering, medicine for the sick, and houses for the destitute, how do Christians respond to the needs of a devastated city? Certainly there is more to rebuilding a city than merely erecting new buildings and filling them with people. Cities need something which technology cannot provide and urban demographers cannot describe. Cities, good cities, require spiritual foundations, and for that they need a word from the Lord. At the heart of the Christian religion lies the assumption that lives, homes, and cities must be built on the foundation of the Word of God, or sooner or later, they will lie as devastated as Managua on the morning after the earthquake. Real urban renewal involves rejection of evil, commitment to good, obedience to God, and hearing God's Word. Ezra and Nehemiah knew that, and on that basis they set to work.

The Reading of the Law and the Renewal of the City

The eighth chapter of Nehemiah's prophecy recounts the returned exiles from Babylon gathered at the Water Gate of the temple in Jerusalem. They were celebrating the Feast of Trumpets, a sacred festival that God had ordained as an annual celebration on the first day of the seventh month (Lev. 23:23-25). It was a "day of solemn rest, a memorial proclaimed with blasts of trumpets, a holy convocation."

Nehemiah, the architect of Jerusalem's urban renewal, had something very special in mind for this day. He had put forward every effort to inspire the people to rebuild the ruined city. They had cleared away the rubble, erected the walls, and built new houses. It had been a tremendous undertaking, and Nehemiah was proud of the people's accomplishments. But something more was needed. Nehemiah realized that moral and religious reforms had to be made to give the nation a spiritual foundation that would set it apart from other nations and prevent the kind of decay that had precipitated its former destruction. For social and political reforms to take hold in a way that would please God and preserve the people, spiritual renewal must occur. This could happen only if God's Word was known, understood, and obeyed.

The public reading of the Scripture every seven years was required by the law of Moses (Deut. 31:9-13). But during the Babylonian captivity this practice, like many others, had not been followed. Before the exile, the religious sensitivities of the people had progressively deteriorated until they were not interested in what the law of God had to say. During the exile, circumstances had not permitted such a religious assembly and the feasts prescribed by Moses could not be held. But now the exiles had returned to their own city, and a chastened people was ready to listen. The returning exiles sincerely desired to hear what God's law had to say.

So it was that Ezra the priest was asked to bring out the law of Moses and read it before the assembly at Jerusalem. Ezra at this time was devoting the major part of his energy to the compilation of a complete edition of the canonical Scriptures, and the opportunity to read them publicly at the Feast of Trumpets filled him with delight. On a wooden platform erected for the occasion, Ezra and thirteen other priests stood like trumpeters before the people. When Ezra grew weary in this Scripture-reading marathon, the other priests would help him. Besides the priests, thirteen Levites were there to help the people understand. As Ezra opened the book, the people rose to their feet as an act of reverence for the Word of God. It was a solemn moment, a turning point in Israel's history. From that day onward, Jerusalem and Israel would never be the same, for the city's renewal acquired a distinctively religious dimension. The ruined city was not only rebuilt, but also reconstituted. "The joy of Jerusalem was heard afar off," reported Nehemiah, and that joy, he well knew, was God's gift to a renewed and obedient people who had heard God's Word and had submitted their lives in conformity to it (Neh. 12:43-47).

Lessons from Scripture for Urban Renewal

Modern apostles to the city can learn valuable lessons from this ancient Scripture. The first is that *the Word of God is never outdated.* It was a long road from rural Sinai, where Moses heard the law, to the postexile city of Jerusalem. The law of Moses was already an old document when Ezra mounted the wooden pulpit and began reading to the people. But the document was not outdated. It spoke to the people and it met their needs. It was relevant, and it accomplished God's purpose in renewing the life of Israel.

The Bible is always relevant, and it speaks to us in our time as powerfully as it did to people centuries ago. There are sound reasons for this. Nobody at any time in history has had to face a truly unique problem. The human race is one race, and men of all ages and nationalities are human beings made by God in his image. God is still the same God; man's sin is still the problem underlying all human disorders, hostilities, and conflicts. Although human problems may come in different sizes and shapes from one generation to another, they are fundamentally the same. It is to this basic and universal sinful human condition that the Bible speaks its message of judgment and redemption. The doctrines that Moses gave to ancient Israel, which the prophets preached to their contemporaries, and which Jesus and the apostles proclaimed in the days of the New Testament, are the doctrines that can bring comfort and hope to modern urbanites. There is no other message worth bringing.

Second, *God's written Word is translatable into every language and culture of mankind*. The word must be spoken and communicated in the languages of the heart, so that its full impact may be felt and understood.

Upon examining Nehemiah 8:1-12, we see that Bible exposition accompanied Bible reading, with the intent that the lay men and women of Israel would understand the law of God. Not only was the Bible *read* clearly and intelligibly, but its message was *explained* by the Levites as the reading went along.

Besides the reading of God's law and the explanation of its meaning, *translation* probably took place as well, for the postexile Jews knew Chaldee, the vernacular dialect used in Babylon, better than they knew pure Hebrew. Likely, some of the Levites gave a running translation of the law, sentence by sentence, so that the people might hear it in Chaldee, the language they knew best.

There is an important principle involved here for urban apostolate in our day. People need to hear God's Word in the language they know best and in the cultural context in which they feel most at home. The Wycliffe Bible Translators, the largest nondenominational missionary organization in the world, accepts this as the basic principle of their entire strategy. Applied to a remote Indian tribe in Latin America, it means that translators must learn the language, translate the Scriptures into that language, and communicate the truth of God's Word through the culture and language of the people. This holds true also in urban centers, which are vast mosaics of human cultures, languages, and characteristics.

In his book *Understanding Church Growth*, Donald A. McGavran says that in some circumstances the key to successful urban apostolate is the multiplication of tribe, caste, and language churches in the metropolitan center. In a few cases, says Dr. McGavran, the melting-pot aspect of cities causes a situation in which large numbers of people from separate tribes, castes, and language groups truly want to leave their past and join together in one language, culture, and congregation. Under such circumstances, united churches representing many different ethnic groups are highly desirable and will promote the gospel. But in situations where the melting-pot aspect of cities has not developed this far, it is a mistake to try to press together into a single congregation people who do not feel at home in such a situation and who will not be able to comprehend the message which they hear because of language and cultural barriers. It is the *understanding* of the Word of God and its application to all of life which must be emphasized. The word-not-understood accomplishes little. The chief business of the church is not to seek to fuse the various elements found in the urban population into one people, but to communicate God's Word in the language and in the cultural forms the people know best. If anyone disagrees with this principle, let him worship with a congregation of whose services he understands only one word in three, and then ask himself how much encouragement and direction from God's Word he received!

Imagine for a moment that you and your companions have spent the night in a remote Indian village high in the mountains of central Mexico. You have come to this village to preach the Word of God. Last night as you lay in your sleeping bag you watched the stars through the cracks in the roof of the dilapidated house in which you are staying. As you lay there listening to the howling of dogs, you wondered about the religion of these Indian people. What a strange combination it is of traditional Catholicism and ancient paganism. And now, in this village, there are the beginnings of true evangelical faith.

Just down the hill stands a magnificent old church which was built in 1742 by Spanish priests using the forced labor of the Indians. It is a Protestant church now, because some years ago the villagers decided to chase out the priest and adopt the teachings and practices of an English missionary who, at the risk of his life, had brought them the gospel. This morning you rose early to conduct your private devotions and prepare your message for the day. You walked down the hill and found the mammoth baptismal font that once had stood inside the church entrance. In their enthusiasm for the new faith and resentment toward the priests who had exploited them, the villagers had destroyed the church's images and rolled the baptismal font out the door and down the hill. Part of it broke off, and now it makes a comfortable chair. You prepared your message this morning sitting in the old baptismal font on the side of the hill.

It is a beautiful day and the people have gathered on the hill just outside the town to listen to you preach. Some of them have come from other villages and walked for several hours over narrow mountain trails. Whole families have come. The women are down in front, while the men, wearing their big sombreros, are farther up the hill. Babies are being nursed and children move to and fro among the women, and you know that you will have to speak as loudly as you can to reach this audience.

The villagers are in for a special treat this morning, for your companion is a Wycliffe Bible translator, and he has brought with him a draft copy of the translation of the New Testament which he has spent twelve years preparing. He is the only white man in the world who speaks the particular dialect of these people. Until now, all the religious instruction they have ever received has been in Spanish, which they understand only in part. Many of them think that God speaks and understands only Spanish.

After a few hymns have been sung with the peculiar lilt which the Indians give to Spanish tunes, your companion stands up and opens his notebook. His voice is not very loud and you wonder how the people in the back are going to hear him. He begins reading from one of Paul's epistles. The language he is using is Mazahuatl. There is a look of astonishment on the faces of the women in the front. A small boy who has run up to his mother demanding something from her is suddenly seized by the shoulder, and the mother clamps her hand tightly over his mouth to keep him quiet. Women quickly press their infants to their breasts to still their whimpering. Heads lean forward. All the way to the back there is almost absolute silence. Calmly the translator reads the Scriptures in Mazahuatl, and the villagers drink in every word as though God were speaking to them directly from heaven. Some begin to weep quietly as God's Word in Mazahuatl sinks into their soul. "Now I know God understands us," an aged grandmother tells you later. "I often wondered if he did." When, after three hours, the service ends, there is a sense of joy, almost exhilaration, as the people cluster around your companion, the Bible translator, and inquire more about God. They have heard God's Word today in their own language, and they have understood its meaning.

"And they read from the book, from the law of God, *clearly*; and they gave the sense, so that the people understood the reading. . . . And all the people went their way to eat and drink and to send portions and to make great *rejoicing*, because they had *understood* the words that were declared to them" (Neh. 8:8, 12, RSV, italics mine). To bring about the urban renewal that he intended, Nehemiah made sure the people *understood* God's Word and its message for their lives. In the vast mosaic of human population which is the city, the same thing must occur today. There is tremendous human diversity within the city, and this diversity must be recognized and accounted for in the communication of God's Word. Every citizen of metropolis needs to hear the gospel in the language he knows best and in a cultural context he understands. Unless this is done, there will not occur that repentant weeping and joyful celebration over the Word of God that are prerequisites of urban renewal.

Issues of the Heart and Society

The third observation on the basis of Nehemiah's strategy for the moral and religious reform of Jerusalem is that the Word of God speaks to the issues of the heart and society. When people understand what God's Word is really saying to them, when they repent on account of its judgments and take heed to its precepts, then endless possibilities open up for the establishment of a society which pleases God and satisfies human needs.

Nehemiah 8:9, 10, says that the Levites "taught the people . . . and all the people wept when they heard the words of the law." They wept because they had sinned. They had broken God's law repeatedly before the exile and had been cut off from its public proclamation in Babylon. Now as they heard it afresh in the gate of the city, it touched their hearts and exposed their shortcomings as never before. The Feast of Trumpets became a day of mourning and public display of repentance. That is precisely what Nehemiah had intended, for the basis of his strategy for urban renewal lay in religious and moral reformation brought about by the exposition of God's Word.

The largest and most modern Protestant church in Mexico is found in the rapidly growing city of Guadalajara, in the hard-core Roman Catholic state of Jalisco. In his book *Church Growth in Mexico*, Donald A. McGavran placed Guadalajara at the top of the list of "conservative cities" in Mexico, and by this he meant cities that for historic, geographic, social, and political reasons had shown themselves unresponsive to the gospel. The church to which I am referring is the "mother church" of the indigenous *Luz del Mundo* movement, sometimes called the "Jesus Only" movement, which was begun around 1940 by a Mexican layman by the name of Joaquin. Joaquin testified that God had changed his name to Aaron and had given him a special revelation to the effect that he was to preach the gospel and place the Scriptures in the hands of the common people.

The mother church in Guadalajara has an auditorium that seats approximately three thousand people, and it was erected without the need for foreign subsidy. The members by and large are humble people—common artisans and factory workers. For the most part they live together in one corner of the city of Guadalajara, and there they put their religion into practice in a most remarkable way. Their emphasis upon the Bible is phenomenal. It is the only book which the ordinary members are permitted to use besides a hymnal. The memorization of Bible texts is the hallmark of every part of their religious activity, and from the smallest child to the oldest grandparent, everyone seems intent upon memorizing and reciting the Bible. In talking with them, one is struck by the fact that "because the Holy Scriptures teach us," is a standard preface to every answer they give concerning their doctrine and life.

Daily Bible instruction is given to all school-age children of the *Luz del Mundo* zone of the city. Even though the Mexican constitution prohibits religious instruction in elementary schools, so influential has this tightly controlled religious community become that special arrangements between the church and local government officials allow the children to be released from the government school for an hour each day to attend Bible classes in the church. Illiteracy is one of the things which the movement despises most, for an illiterate person cannot read the Bible. So emphatic are they about the importance of Bible reading, that theirs is the only municipal district in the state of Jalisco that has no illiterates. In order to honor the people of the area for this singular accomplishment, the government has awarded them a white flag, symbol of total literacy. This flag is proudly displayed in the park near the church.

Worship services are held at the central church seven days a week, and the Sunday services range from two to three hours in length. A distinctive feature of these services is the degree of audience participation, especially through the recitation of Scripture. So schooled are these people in the Scriptures that as soon as the speaker on the platform begins to quote a Bible verse, the whole audience breaks out in unison and helps him finish it. Preaching takes on an antiphonal quality with the audience very much involved in the proclamation. The overall effect is awesome. Again we see the important role which the Bible plays in the *Luz del Mundo* movement, as the members seek to remain true to Joaquin's original vision. Without the emphasis upon daily Scripture memorization from childhood to old age, this kind of group participation in formal worship would be impossible.

The reason I mention the *Luz del Mundo* movement in our study of Nehemiah 8 is because these people have achieved a remarkably high standard of urban life on the basis of their single-minded adherence to the moral and religious precepts of the Bible. Any taxicab driver in the city of Guadalajara will testify to the moral difference between the area of the city occupied by the "Jesus people" and the rest of the urban center. There are no taverns, saloons, or houses of prostitution in their area. Brawling, fighting between families, and drunkenness are virtually unknown. The streets are safe, clean, and tranquil. The women are dressed modestly and the children are well behaved. The men are known for industriousness and honesty in their work. Even their severest critics admit that these people put religion into practice.

The teaching of the Bible is the key factor in the movement, but to complete the picture we must take this one step further. *The Bible in the hands of laymen* expresses more completely the source of the movement's strength. The movement has put the Bible into the hands of the laity and it has turned the laity loose to teach one another, edify one another, and witness to the world. The emphasis in all the services, in the children's classes, and in the discussions is on the meaning and practical application of the plain teaching of Scripture. It is this kind of biblical exposition—sometimes erroneous, often simplistic, and yet dynamic in its practical effect—which has made the qualitative difference in the area of the city where the *Luz del Mundo* people live.

This is essentially what Ezra and Nehemiah were seeking to accomplish in the life of restored Jerusalem. Their goal was the total reformation of Jewish society according to the Word of God. The renewal of urban life and the society of the nation were to be accomplished through the Scriptures read, explained, understood, and applied. The social reforms that Nehemiah describes in the rest of the book would not have occurred without the Law being read and explained. Whereas Jerusalem's pre-exile false prophets were largely responsible for the spiritual decay of the nation (Jer. 23:15), the purpose of Nehemiah and those with him was to disseminate the true knowledge of God's law. For when the people understood the full message of that law, they would tremble, rejoice, and be renewed.

Celebration in the City

Upon hearing the law of God, the people were moved to worship and celebration. Nehemiah the governor, Ezra the priest and scribe, and the Levites who taught the people said:

> ". . . This day is holy to the Lord your God; do not mourn or weep. . . . Go your way, eat the fat and drink sweet wine and send portions to him for whom nothing is prepared; for this day is holy to our Lord; and do not be grieved, for the joy of the Lord is your strength" (Neh. 8:9, 10, RSV).

When they heard this, the people ate and drank, and sent portions to the needy. There was great rejoicing because "they had understood the words that were declared to them" (v. 12).

The joy of the Lord comes to those who know God's Word and understand it, and it then becomes their strength to undertake great things. The Word slays and also restores. We rise from our knees to lives of noble service.

The renewal of the city and reformation of urban life wait for the regeneration of human hearts through the Word of God. Here is found the vital significance of urban pulpits, which can accomplish more toward the renewal of urban life through the faithful exposition of God's Word than any other instrument or platform. Here is also the clue to dynamic urban mission, which depends upon the heralding of "Thus saith the Lord," and the communication of God's Word to the city.

The New York International Bible Society sponsors the "Bible Brigades." From New York City's red-light district to affluent New Jersey suburbs, these "Bible Brigades" distribute the printed Scriptures door-to-door. Armed with Scripture portions and printed invitations to attend nearby sponsoring churches, Christian volunteers enter both X-rated hotels and plush residential areas, testifying to God's transforming power in their lives and inviting others to read the Scriptures and follow the Lord. In the past twenty years, this program has distributed more than 5 million Scripture portions to homes housing some 20 million people.

The coordinator of this Scripture distribution program, Bruno A. Militano, says that their focus is on the family and their aim is to plant the Scriptures in the place where the family has its center, the individual home. This family-centered program began in 1950 as an experiment in fourteen Harlem neighborhoods which were pinpointed by the police as breeding grounds for gang warfare. The New York International Bible Society invited local churches to provide volunteers to work with Society agents in taking Spanish and English language Scripture booklets to every home in the beleaguered neighborhoods. To encourage fellowship and follow-up, each Scripture packet carried a message inviting the recipients to attend a nearby church.

The program was begun as an experiment in some of New York City's most difficult areas, and it proved so successful that it has

54

spread to other urban communities in New York, New Jersey, Pennsylvania, Connecticut, Massachusetts, Maine, and even to the city of Calgary in Alberta, Canada. Militano estimates that seventeen hundred churches have participated in the program, sending out some twelve thousand volunteers of all ages. Scriptures have been distributed in a variety of languages ranging from Yiddish to Japanese, and the results have been encouraging.

The joy of salvation has become a reality in the lives of hundreds of individuals and their families through the work of these "foot soldiers" of the Lord. A Baptist church in the infamous Brownsville section of Brooklyn reported some time ago that forty adults joined the church following a family-to-family campaign in their area and one hundred children were added to the Sunday school. A Spanish Pentecostal church in Brooklyn, and a Baptist church in Spanish Harlem baptized twenty-four adults at the conclusion of a Bible distribution campaign.

The manager of an Eighth Avenue hotel tells of two prostitutes who were residents in his hotel and whom he could not evict because they regularly paid their rent. When family-to-family volunteers visited the hotel the women received the gospel message from the lips of the volunteers, read the Scriptures privately, were converted, and subsequently gave up their immoral profession. The hotel owner, though not converted himself, was pleased that at last the women had left his hotel and was awed by the obvious change in their lives. He observed: "That book certainly did something to them that I couldn't do."

What renewal in the city there would be if Christians by the tens of thousands, with ministers of the gospel in the lead, would fan out across the neighborhoods and barrios, towering apartments and seething slums, distributing God's Word, explaining its contents, translating its message into the languages and cultures of urban people, and making themselves instruments of God for the salvation of souls and the transformation of urban life.

Prob being - these were a special people of Θ - who would respond in hope bec of relatshp.

Chapter 4

Barnabas

The Making of a Missionary Church

Antioch of Syria was a cosmopolitan city, closer in character to a modern metropolis than any other city in the Roman world. Antioch is crucial for a biblical perception of urban mission, because patterns were established at Antioch that set the course of mission history and changed the religious map of the world. At Antioch, the gospel first began to be preached to people who had no previous connection with the Jewish faith and community. The church at Antioch, by commissioning and sending out the first missionaries to the unevangelized world, became the mother of all the Gentile churches. Furthermore, in the life and ministry of the Antiochan church, a man who was destined to become the great urban apostle of the first century learned firsthand what a Gentile church could be, and this lesson made an indelible stamp on his career.

Beauty, Idolatry, and Sin

As cities go, Antioch had everything to offer. Under Roman rule, it was the third city of the Empire, the capital of the province of Syria, and was governed by a proconsul in charge of two legions of soldiers. Known as "Antioch the Beautiful," the city undertook a tremendous building program, which was financed jointly by Augustus and Herod. Its athletic stadiums drew thousands to see the annual games. Antioch was the center for diplomatic relations with Rome's vassal states in the East, and was a meeting point for many nationalities and cultures. It was a place where East and West met each other, a truly cosmopolitan center. Every religious movement in the ancient world was represented in Antioch. There were the cults of Zeus and Apollo and the rest of the Greek pantheon. There were also the Syrian worship of Baal and the Mother Goddess and the mystery religions with their teachings on death and resurrection, initiation, and salvation. Occultism was common along with magic, witchcraft, and astrology. Archeological excavations in and around the city indicate that every religion of ancient times had followers in Antioch.

Antioch was also known for its immorality. The lurid dancing girls of Antioch were the talk of the Mediterranean world. As a large, rich, commercial center, Antioch embodied the voluptuousness and corruption of a pagan society untouched by Christian influence. The city rivaled Corinth as a center for vice, and the Roman poet Juvenal, writing near the end of the first century A.D., charged that the wickedness of Antioch was one of the sources of Rome's corruption.

Despite these negative features, Antioch became the main gateway of the gospel to the Gentile world. It is interesting to note that the New Testament never talks about Antioch's wickedness and idolatry, its culture and beauty, or its importance as one of the great commercial centers of antiquity. In describing Antioch, Luke refers only to the great spiritual events that took place in the city. Events in Antioch affected the course of the gospel, threw open the Empire to evangelization, and molded the character of the missionary enterprise. As for impact upon the world, Antioch soon came to supersede Jerusalem and developed into the missionary headquarters of the first century.

A Church of Unknown Origins

Just when and how the gospel first arrived in Antioch, no one knows. The Book of Acts tells us that when the disciples of Jesus were scattered because of the persecution that arose in connection with Stephen's martyrdom, some of them came to Antioch. It is possible that there was already a believing community in Antioch before Stephen died. This church, which did so much to change the religious map of the Roman Empire, was founded by some unknown missionary, probably a layman who, without publicity or recognition, was faithful to the Lord. Maybe it was

Nicolaus, one of the first deacons at Jerusalem, who came from Antioch and may have decided earlier to return home and spread the Good News among his fellow proselytes (Acts 6:5). In any case, we are not told who it was that first preached the gospel in Antioch, or under what conditions he labored.

Most of the churches of the first century, and all succeeding centuries, were founded by Christians whose names were never recorded in history books. They received no acclaim, on earth at least, for their labors and sacrifices. Some giants of faith and missionary endeavor stand out against the horizons of history, and we all know their names: William Carey, Hudson Taylor, David Livingstone. Their very names call to mind the opening of great areas of the world to the gospel. We thank God for such people, for they were faithful servants and God used them mightily. But at the same time we must remember that the vast majority of converts, and most Christian churches, were the fruits of an anonymous multitude who never made the history books but who served God faithfully without earthly acclaim. It was that way at Antioch. We do not know who began the church, but Christians for centuries have benefited from what he or she did.

Racial and Ethnic Barriers Overcome

Luke records that when persecution broke out in Jerusalem, the disciples of Jesus were scattered as far as Phoenicia, Cyprus, and Antioch. As they fled, they spoke of their faith to none except Jews (Acts 11:19). We can understand the racial and ethnic narrowness of their evangelism when we remember how reluctant most people are today to bridge the gaps between different communities and to witness cross-culturally, even after nineteen centuries of Christian growth and instruction.

"But there were some of them, men of Cyprus and Cyrene, who on coming to Antioch spoke to the Greeks also, preaching the Lord Jesus" (Acts 11:20). That was the breakthrough! The earlier preaching of Philip to the Samaritans and the Ethiopian proselyte, and Peter's encounter with Cornelius the centurion, remarkable events as they were in themselves, still had to do with people who belonged to the circle of Jewish faith and piety. But at Antioch pagans heard the gospel from Christian lips, and the universality of the gospel era began to take shape.

59

The cosmopolitan climate of the city was conducive to this kind of breakthrough. Antioch was at one and the same time a Hellenistic city, a Roman city, and a Jewish city. It was the meeting place of Oriental and Greek civilizations. It had a large Jewish population, but religiously many of the Jews were lax, and social barriers between Jews and Gentiles were relatively small. Some of the Jews themselves were engaged in proselyting efforts, and converts to Judaism were numerous. If the gap between the Jewish and Gentile worlds was to be bridged anywhere, it could be expected to happen in this cosmopolitan center.

In his book *Evangelism in the Early Church*, Michael Green reminds us that it was not the official policy of the Jerusalem church to evangelize Antioch. On the contrary, it was a spontaneous movement arising from Christian people who could not keep quiet about Jesus their Lord.[1] Green points out that Antioch of Syria was almost a microcosm of Roman antiquity in the first century, a city which encompassed most of the advantages, the problems, and the human interests with which the new faith would have to grapple as it moved across the world. The racial and ethnic issues were certainly two of the most fundamental, and in this area the Holy Spirit led the church of Antioch in a direction of highest importance for the spread of the gospel.

Evangelistic Revival and Careful Follow-Up

Two unnamed Christians, foreigners to the great city, began preaching "Jesus is Lord" with tremendous results. There were many "gods" and many "lords" in the Gentile world, but for these followers of Jesus there was only one God, the Maker of heaven and earth; and only one Lord, Jesus Christ, through whom all things were made and who himself had come into the world to reconcile sinners to God. The hand of the Lord was with them, and a great number of people believed and turned to the Lord (Acts 11:21). All the important things that the Antiochan church did later must be seen against the background of the evangelistic fire that broke loose in the city when the gospel of Jesus Christ was first preached to the Gentiles. Before Antioch reached out in mercy to the needy, or commissioned some of

---

[1] Michael Green, *Evangelism in the Early Church* (Grand Rapids: William B. Eerdmans Publishing Co., 1970), p. 114.

their own leaders to carry the gospel to faraway places, the church learned to evangelize powerfully and fruitfully in its own city streets.

News of these occurrences reached the ears of the church in Jerusalem and the church sent a one-man commission, in the person of Barnabas, to find out what was happening. At this early stage in the church's history, Jerusalem still had great influence, and we can imagine how the disciples in Antioch felt when they heard that Jerusalem was sending someone to investigate their movement. They probably thought: "Here comes trouble!" Jerusalem was the mother church, the citadel of Jewish conservatism. Things did not go the same way in Antioch as they did in Jerusalem, and the new Gentile converts brought to the church faces and practices which Jerusalem could hardly imagine. What would Barnabas be like? Would he take back to Jerusalem a negative report? Would he condemn this exciting new breakthrough of the gospel into the Gentile world and oppose its spreading any further?

"When he [Barnabas] arrived," says Luke, "and saw the evidence of the grace of God, he was glad and encouraged them all to remain true to the Lord with all their hearts. For he was a good man, full of the Holy Spirit and faith" (Acts 11:23-24a, NIV). What a relief it must have been to the Antiochan church that Barnabas was the kind of man that he was. One of the hardest things to understand in religious work is the attitude of some of God's children who, when they see something beautiful happening, oppose it, criticize it, and refuse to have anything to do with it. But Barnabas was not such a person. When he saw the evidence of God's grace at work transforming people's lives, he rejoiced, recognized its potential, and threw his energies into the follow-up program. Barnabas realized that the devil would soon begin to discourage the new converts and lead them back into sin and idolatry. The fruits of the Antiochan revival needed to be consolidated immediately or much would be lost. Barnabas apparently did not even take time to go back to Jerusalem with his report. Maybe he sent the elders a letter, but the Bible does not say. All we know is that he set to work at once and "a great number of people were brought to the Lord" (Acts 11:24, NIV).

Church growth can occur in three different ways. First, there can be *biological* church growth, by which we mean the enlargement of the church through internal growth—children born into Christian homes and brought up in the covenant community to acknowledge God in their whole walk of life. Church growth of this kind is important and it represents God's age-old way of dealing with believing parents and their children from one generation to another. The second kind of church growth is what we call *transfer* growth. It takes place when church members move from one location to another and in the new location either join an established church or begin a new one. As far as any numerical addition to the church of Jesus Christ is concerned, nothing has happened. There is no net increase. Christians have simply transferred their membership from one community of believers to another.

The third kind of church growth is the kind that took place at Antioch. We call it *conversion* growth. Granted, in the beginning there was some transfer growth at Antioch as refugees arrived from Jerusalem, but the really important factor in Antioch was the number of pagans who were converted to Christian convictions and church membership. That is the kind of growth we must look for in evangelism. When, due to uncertainty or frustration, people engaged in mission work begin to minimize the importance of winning converts from unbelief to saving faith in Christ, something has seriously gone wrong. The pattern established at Antioch was followed consistently by Paul and the rest of the apostles. They verbally proclaimed the Good News of the Lord Jesus for the purpose of persuading men and women to believe the message and be converted to the Lord. Anything less than this is a serious departure from the New Testament pattern of evangelism.

Barnabas was a teacher and organizer. He recognized what the Antiochan church needed most at that time: encouragement, instruction, and counseling in the direction they ought to go. Barnabas realized too that the increasing number of converts meant that he could not handle the follow-up alone, so he went to look for Saul, the gifted young convert from Pharisaism whom he had introduced to the apostles at Jerusalem (Acts 9:27). This decision on the part of Barnabas to look for Saul of Tarsus and bring him to Antioch to help in the teaching ministry was crucial both for Antioch and for the spread of the faith throughout the Empire. Barnabas probably did not realize that he was recruiting for active ministry a man whose preaching, writing, and personal influence in the providence of God would change the course of history.[2]

Paul's experience at Antioch provided him with a model of what the church should be. It was a model which later he set out to duplicate, not rigidly or without allowance for differences required by local customs and circumstances, but still with its basic contours visibly intact.

For Paul, Antioch remained the place where he had seen what the Gentile church could be. It was there that he learned what it meant to bring Gentiles to a saving faith in Jesus Christ and instruct, guide, and work with them until a strong, functioning church had been established. Antioch did more to mold Paul than most people realize. A great deal of what we have come to recognize as the Pauline strategy of church planting, (and the theology which accompanies it), can be traced to his early experiences with the vibrant young church at Antioch.

Critics Called Them Christians

In the ancient world, slaves were called by their master's name, and that probably explains how the followers of the Lord first came to be called *cristianoi* ("Christians"). Slaves really had no will of their own; they could only obey orders. Their names were derived from the persons who owned them, and they could not hold property or leave an inheritance. They were their own masters in nothing, but in everything they submitted to a higher authority, that of their master and lord.

The Bible does not record the name of the observant critic who first gave disciples the nickname, "Christians." But the name stuck because it fit. Disciples of Jesus regarded him as their Master and themselves as his slaves. "We are not our own," they said, "for we have been bought with a price." Body and soul, in life and in death, they belonged to their divine Master, Jesus

---

[2] The question may be asked whether Barnabas had learned of the prophecy made at the time of Paul's conversion concerning his future ministry (cf. Acts 9:15; 22:21; 26:18). If Barnabas was already aware of God's intention with Paul, then he may have recognized in Antioch the very situation that would launch Paul on the Gentile mission to which God had appointed him.

Christ. Doing God's will was their chief concern. The sovereignty of God was more than a slogan or a doctrine. It had a decisive influence on their way of life, and the enemies of the gospel took note and called them "Christians."

The apostle Paul learned much about the character and purpose of the Christian life by observing and working with the young church at Antioch. He took up the derogatory title given to followers of Jesus and made it his badge of honor. He introduced himself to the Romans as "Paul, a bondservant of Christ Jesus, called to be an apostle and set apart for the gospel of God" (Rom. 1:1). The "bondservant" status of Christ's followers echoes throughout all of Paul's writings. Christians have no abiding citizenship or inheritance on earth. Their home is in heaven. The purpose of life is service to God, and whether they live or die, they belong to him. The mark of the Antiochan believers became the definition of discipleship for all times.

Today there is a growing awareness that the major reason for the church's powerlessness in the secular city is the lack of true discipleship on the part of most church members. Few merit the name "Christian, bondslave of Jesus Christ." Materialism has made church members virtually indistinguishable from the rest of mankind. The world's way of thinking and doing has by and large taken over, and consequently the church has little to say, with credibility at least, to the secular city. This is a generalization—thank God, there are exceptions. But no honest and informed observer can deny that the supreme need of the church is a radical rediscovery of what it means to be Christian.

 Is it not principally in the teaching ministry that we have failed in evangelism? Significantly, the phrase, "and in Antioch the disciples were for the first time called Christians," follows immediately after the statement: "For a whole year they [Barnabas and Saul] met with the church, and taught a large company of people" (Acts 11:26). Without a thorough teaching ministry, the Antiochan believers would not have matured into the kind of people their critics dubbed "Christians." And no urban strategy today can be expected to produce great fruits unless it includes in-depth instruction in the Scriptures, Christian life, and discipleship.

Compassion Toward Needy Saints

While visting a small chapel in Brazil I observed the clothing which some of the children wore. It was the winter season and fairly cold. Toes stuck through the tips of some of the children's shoes, and a few barefoot ones kept their feet curled beneath them, partly perhaps because of the cold and partly out of embarrassment because they had no shoes. These children came from Christian homes; homes where the fathers worked ten to twelve hours a day, six days a week, to earn a living for their families; homes where mothers did everything possible to feed their children and clothe them adequately against the cold. When I looked at the coats worn by the two girls sitting next to me I realized that my Black Labrador at home in Michigan had better things to sleep on than these little girls could wear to church.

What would the Antiochan Christians do if they were informed of Christians suffering in a faraway place? Well, what *did* they do? Luke tells us that when they learned that a great famine would sweep over the world and their brethren were already suffering in Judea, they "determined, every one according to his ability, to send relief to the brethren who lived in Judea" (Acts 11:29, RSV). While not denying that Christians have obligations to help needy people indiscriminately, the believers at Antioch sensed that their first duty was toward needy saints. The Old Testament teaching that among God's people there should be mutual sharing and relief of poverty had been made clear to them by their teachers (Deut. 15). As a result, the believers did not have to be scolded or pled with. Once the needs of the Judean believers were presented, they responded generously.

This kind of voluntary sharing between believers had taken place in Jerusalem from the very beginning. In Acts 2:44-47 (NIV), the life of the early Christians is described as follows:

> All the believers were together and had everything in common. Selling their possessions and goods, they gave to anyone as he had need. Every day they continued to meet together in the temple courts. They broke bread in their homes and ate together with glad and sincere hearts, praising God and enjoying the favor of all the people. And the Lord added to their number daily those who were being saved.

Acts 4:32-35 gives a similar picture of early church life. What is described here was not an early form of communism of the kind propagated by Karl Marx and his followers. Nowhere does the Bible teach that it is wrong to own property, or that the Christian community should take over its members' private possessions and own them collectively. On the contrary, early Christians were free to use their possessions as their consciences directed them. If they felt led to sell their land so that the money obtained might assist the poor, such sales were acceptable. Sales of this kind would not have been condoned if private ownership of land and other such possessions were wrong in principle. What we see in the New Testament are not prohibitions against private ownership of land and property, but the voluntary sale of excess possessions on the part of wealthier Christians to meet the material needs of their poorer brethren.

The apostle Paul saw what the Antiochan churches did, and his own hands helped convey their gift to Jerusalem, where it was administered under the supervision of the elders of the church. Later, when Paul was on his missionary journeys, he taught by his preaching and writing that the support of the saints was a primary Christian responsibility. II Corinthians 8 deals with the "gracious work" (vv. 7, 19) of Christian charity toward needy brethren. In Paul's theology and mission strategy, word and deed ministries were not separated, nor administered separately by different agencies. They were integrated both in the church and in the apostolic mission.

The Strength of a Balanced Church

There was a balance in the ministry of the Antiochan church. Luke wrote that in the church at Antioch there were "prophets and teachers" (Acts 13:1). In this situation, prophets most likely were those who spoke God's truth to the unsaved, to inquirers, and to those who were coming to Christ from Jewish or pagan backgrounds. Teachers were those who deepened the faith of the new believers through instruction and helped the young believers mature in their understanding of the Scriptures and the practice of the Christian life. Merrill C. Tenney says of the church at Antioch that it was the home of both great Christian preaching and the headquarters of evangelistic missions. From this center of both teaching and proclamation, the missionary fire spread across the Empire.[3]

This balance between evangelistic proclamation and patient, thorough instruction was vital to the health and growth of the church. We see throughout the New Testament that evangelism and teaching were not separated in the apostolic mission. Paul's teaching ministry is referred to repeatedly (Acts 11:26; 15:35; 18:11; 20:20; 28:31), and the apostle called himself a teacher (I Tim. 2:7; II Tim. 1:11). The epistles were part of Paul's teaching ministry, and it was characteristic of the apostolic ministry that evangelism and nurture were maintained in lively balance.

There was also balance in the spiritual life of the church. Worship, fasting, and prayer were earmarks of the community that God chose to use mightily for the spread of the gospel. Great missionary movements can always be traced to people on their knees, and there has never been a church that accomplished significant things for God that was not strong internally and spiritually.

The clearest evidence of Antioch's strength was its readiness to be a sending church, the first missionary-sending church of the New Testament era. From Jerusalem witnesses were forcibly "scattered abroad" (Acts 11:19), but from Antioch apostles were set apart, commissioned, and sent forth to the work (Acts 13:2). Such sending was, and still is, the sign of a vibrant and obedient church.

In Acts, the church is the object of missions, the agent of missions, and the source of mission personnel. The immediate goal of the apostles was to plant churches wherever they went. No evangelistic effort was regarded as successful unless a community of disciples, a church, was established. At the same time, the church itself was God's special agency of evangelism in every city and region, and from the church missionary personnel were called. The apostles' whole strategy was built around this concept of the missionary nature and responsibility of the church.

The apostles whom the Antiochan church commissioned never forgot the special relationship they had to this congregation. When their first missionary journey was completed they came

---

[3] Merrill C. Tenney, *New Testament Survey* (Grand Rapids: William B. Eerdmans Publishing Co., 1961), p. 253.

back to Antioch where, Luke affectionately records, "they had been commended to the grace of God for the work which they had fulfilled" (Acts 14:26, RSV). When the missionaries arrived, "they gathered the church together and declared all that God had done with them, and how he had opened a door of faith to the Gentiles" (Acts 14:27, RSV). Luke says that they stayed "no little time" with the believers in Antioch, and the "home service" ministry of the apostles must have been a great blessing to the church. It is still true that when a church adds an international dimension to its ministry by sending and supporting overseas workers, the spiritual growth, joy, and vitality of the church's own life are greatly enriched.

Antioch left an indelible mark on first-century Christianity. It was there that Barnabas and Paul gained experience in urban ministry. The city of Antioch was a microcosm of everything the two apostles later confronted on their missionary journeys. The church that was founded in Antioch was a model that served them well as they traveled from city to city, preaching the gospel and establishing believers in the faith.

The experience in cross-cultural evangelism, the multi-racial face of the Antiochan church, the concern of believers for suffering brethren in other places, and above all their single-minded devotion to Christ and his service, demonstrated what God's grace could do in a highly urban and pagan environment. To the leaders of such a church the Spirit spoke, commanding them to set apart two of their own number to perform a special work for God in distant places. Through this gateway the gospel went forth to other cities, where the struggles and victories of Antioch were repeated over and over again.

Chapter 5

Paul

The Urban Strategist — His Message

Probably no one in modern history knows more about cities than the modern scholar, Lewis Mumford. Mumford has studied urban life from every angle: from the ancient origins of the city, to its transformations in the course of time, its contemporary forms and structures, and its prospects for the future.[1] Believing that the world is standing on the brink of chaos and only a global conversion to some vital faith can hold mankind back from the fatal plunge, Mumford pleads for a transformation of urban life. With missionary passion, he urges that people everywhere accept a new plan for their lives, a transformation that is the only alternative to global tragedy. It is unfortunate, however, that the transformation for which Mumford pleads is little more than a faith in some sort of democratic love, a dream that can never be fulfilled through human endeavor. We hear Mumford pleading for his "gospel" in his book, *The Conduct of Life*:

> We know that the living places of our planet may be wiped out, and our planet itself denuded of life, through the wholesale misapplication of scientific power unless the change that alters the condition of modern man and the direction of his activities takes

---

[1] Mumford's most outstanding work about the city is *The City in History: Its Origins, Its Transformations, and Its Prospects* (New York: Harcourt, Brace & World, Harbinger Books, 1961). It has been translated into many foreign languages and served as the basis of six documentary films by the National Film Board of Canada, "Lewis Mumford on the City," which have been shown throughout the world.

place in much shorter order: almost, as one reckons historic time, within the twinkling of an eye. . . . How can this be done? By looking not for a single transforming agent, but for millions upon millions of them, in every walk of society, in every country: a democratic transformation, dispersed and widespread, to replace those centralized and authoritarian images which would today, under our current nihilism, be either ineffectual or tyrannous. Let us confess it: such a change has never yet taken place in the past. . . . Today each one of us must turn the light of the lantern inward upon himself; and while he stays at his post performing the necessary work of the day, he must direct every habit and act and duty into a new channel: that which will bring about unity and love. Unless each one of us makes this obligation a personal one, the change that must swiftly be brought about cannot be effected. But all of this is beyond historical precedent and probability? Granted. An impossible dream? No . . . only one thing is needful: faith in the dream itself; for the very ability to dream is the first condition of the dream's realization. And which is better? Think into a nightmare, equally self-fabricated, though we close our eyes to our own constant part in this pathological process—the nightmare of extermination, incineration, and universal death?—or to dream of the alternative processes that will endow individual men and the race at large with a new plan of life? Better the possible self-deception of this dream than the grim fact of that nightmare.[2]

Mumford's impassioned plea is enough to make you weep when you consider how little hope he offers to modern civilization. He calls for radical, personal conversion on the part of millions of people in all walks of life and in every country of the world. Yet he admits that the solution he offers is irrational and lies beyond all historical precedent and probability. The only conclusion we can draw from it is that there is really no hope for the world's great cities, no alternative to the nightmare which is coming.

---

[2] Lewis Mumford, *The Conduct of Life* (New York: Harcourt, Brace and Company, 1951), pp. 118-20.

Paul's "New Creatures in Christ Jesus"

Paul's response to urban despair was the message of reconciliation with God through Jesus Christ. "Therefore, if any one is in Christ, he is a new creation; the old has passed away, behold, the new has come" (II Cor. 5:17, RSV). All this, said Paul, is from God, who through Christ reconciled us to himself and has passed on to us the ministry of reconciliation. The ministry of reconciliation, God in the flesh reconciling the world to himself, was the content of Paul's mission and his message to the urban centers of the Roman world.

Spurred on to a large degree by the fear and despair to which Mumford referred and the longing of mankind for a new social order, many scholars today are demonstrating renewed interest in the biblical concepts of renewal, liberation, restoration, and reconciliation. Often this takes the form of a reinterpretation of the traditional meaning of these terms. We must confess that all too often the church's understanding of biblical concepts has been influenced by self-centered interests. But at the same time we must recognize that in the present situation social ideologies and political concerns are adding a great deal of input as far as modern interpretations of reconciliation are concerned. Liberation theology is foremost in this area.

Young intellectuals, led by Marxists and neo-Marxists, level a great deal of criticism against the church for what they conceive to be the church's self-centeredness and lack of concern. At the same time, Third World nations are asking what Christianity can do to improve their desperate situations. What does the biblical doctrine of reconciliation have to say about peace and social justice? If the apostle Paul were here today, what would his message be concerning urban poverty, injustice, and oppression?

Major changes are occurring in churches' conceptions of their mission and message to the world. There is a shift from personal and experiential understanding of the gospel to communal and social concerns. There is a change from the vertical emphasis in the Christian message to the horizontal. Whereas in the past the horizontal was often neglected, today the vertical is increasingly ignored. We are told that in response to the question "Are you saved?" we should not answer by talking about heaven, but

71

about this world and the changes we want to bring about here and now.

There is, furthermore, a shift from concern over the church as institution to an emphasis upon the church as part of the world. The new theology tells us that God's concern is not limited to the church, nor is it primarily for the church, but for the world. Christ's kingdom is not church-bound, nor is his kingship limited to the community of his followers. Rather, Christ's kingdom is found wherever men are being liberated, where peace is established, and oppression eliminated. This, in terms of the new theology, is the meaning of reconciliation.

The social implications of reconciliation are now of foremost concern. We are told that reconciliation must be *practiced* in the world to be of any value. In this context, conversion is not a change of mind or heart as far as a person's convictions and relationship to God are concerned, but a commitment to join what is understood to be God's program of change for the world. It means commitment to social and political revolution, the elimination of injustice, and the relief of the oppressed.

For those well acquainted with Paul's missionary message all of this sounds strange and unfamiliar. The essential truth of reconciliation as a change in relationship between the sinner and God is missing. According to Paul's writings, man's relationship with God is still basic. If we move away from that, we are left with something other than biblical Christianity. It is certainly true that reconciliation has many practical implications for life, and admittedly the church has not emphasized these as it should. But the primary focus is still *peace with God*, and that is the heart of the Christian message to the city.

Citizenship in the kingdom of heaven is the number one priority in Christian proclamation. Christians have a responsibility in all areas of life, and the implications of reconciliation are far greater than the church generally has realized. Such matters as unjust social structures and the oppression that results from racial prejudice embodied in practices such as apartheid, racial discrimination, and similar wrongs in society, must all engage our attention. They should be objects of our righteous wrath, and their eradication should be a high priority goal of the Christian community. But after acknowledging all this and confessing our past failures to apply the gospel consistently to the wrongs in

72

society, the truth must be reiterated that reconciliation with God is the heart of the gospel and the fountain from which emerges the direction and motivation for God-honoring social changes. If this truth is lost, then the church really cannot say anything new òr important to the world.

Paul's message of reconciliation with God through the person and work of Jesus Christ is seen in his sermon in Antioch (Acts 13:16-41). Paul anchored his message in the Old Testament Scriptures. He began by tracing God's gracious dealings with Israel, leading up to the greatest gift of all, Jesus the Savior (v. 23). Paul appealed to the Hellenistic Jews of the Dispersion to do what the Jews at Jerusalem had failed to do, namely, recognize that Jesus was the Messiah, the fulfillment of Old Testament prophecies, and believe this word of salvation that Paul preached. There was in Paul's message enthusiasm for his mission and optimism concerning its final outcome. He quoted the prophet Habakkuk, saying,"let scoffers beware, for God is doing a great work in our day which those who perish will not believe even when it is told them" (Acts 13:41).

Paul's preaching at Antioch indicates the pattern of his preaching throughout his missionary career. When his audience was acquainted with the Old Testament, he began on that basis and moved quickly to the good news about Christ. When, as at Athens, his hearers lacked the Old Testament background, he began on the common ground of creation and the "seed of religion" that all men possess. At Athens Paul first dealt with matters such as who God is, how God is related to mankind, what God wants all men to do, and why their response to the message was urgent (Acts 17:22-31). But with Jews and proselytes who knew the Old Testament and accepted its authority, Paul could hasten at once to Christ's death and resurrection as the fulfillment of prophecy and God's way of reconciling sinners to himself.[3]

---

[3] Paul's sermon at Athens appears to be incomplete. Acts 17:32 suggests that his hearers began to sneer and disrupt his preaching when Paul spoke of the resurrection. Any missionary who has preached on the street or in places where he did not enjoy the benefit of a formal platform, church decor, or a public address system, knows that hostile crowds can easily disrupt an evangelistic address. The only wise course for the evangelist to take is to make an orderly exit and deal privately with those in the audience who are sincerely interested in what he is teaching. This is precisely what Paul did (vv. 33, 34).

There is no way to read Paul's sermons and avoid the conclusion that he believed that apart from the cross and the
resurrection there was no reconciliation with God or hope for
mankind. This theme flowed through all of Paul's writings as
well. Through suffering and death Christ established his power
and dominion over all satanic powers (cf. Col. 2:15). His death
was a propitiation for all our sins (cf. Rom. 3:25). Preaching and
miracles were not enough, for he had to bear the sins of his
people (cf. Rom. 5:9; Heb. 9:26-28). Without the shedding of
Christ's blood there was no remission of sins (Heb. 9:22). We
were reconciled to God through the payment of a price, and the
price was Christ's atoning death (cf.I Cor. 6:20; 7:23). The oldest
Christian confession, recorded in Paul's own words, points to the
heart of the gospel as reconciliation through Christ's atonement:
"Christ died for our sins according to the Scriptures, he was
buried and rose again the third day, according to the Scriptures"
(I Cor. 15:3, 4). That was the message Paul preached consistently
to the urban world of his day.

If the church loses touch with Paul's doctrine of reconciliation,
then it has lost its message for the world, and whatever it may say
about social and communal relationships will amount to nothing.
When the Christian mission stops talking about God; when it
stops talking about Christ, his death, and his resurrection; when
it stops calling men to repent from their sins and be reconciled to
their Maker, then everything else it says will be valueless.

The Effects of Reconciliation on the World

Each time that a soul finds peace with God, fresh liberating
power is released in the world. Through reconciliation a person is
released from the bondage of sin and death and set free *in the
world* to live a new and transformed life. Reconciliation is from
above, and it has far-reaching effects here on earth. It is all by
grace, not works; of God, not man. And at the same time it affects
every human relationship, every activity, and every level of society.

For too long Christians have concentrated on the individual
and personal dimensions of reconciliation while neglecting the
social implications. If we mean what we say about Christ's lordship over all of life, we must be willing to carry his banner into all

74

of life. Christ's lordship should be the focus of supreme allegiance for the reconciled. This means that Christians should judge everything by a new standard: the criterion of God's Word. Social institutions, economic systems, and traditions of all kinds come under the scrutiny of Christ's standard. This was the thrust of Paul's whole message as he proclaimed the gospel of reconciliation to individuals living in a sin-ridden society. He expected that message to eventually permeate every aspect of Roman life.

Too many Christians today have lost their faith in the power of the gospel. They forget that the future belongs not to the devil but to the Lord. The world is not consciously waiting for Christ's coming but is nonetheless struggling for justice and peace, which only Christ can give. This underscores the truth of what Paul wrote in Romans 8, where he spoke of the "birth pangs" of creation, longing for the new order that Christ would someday establish. To this day God continues to write in men's hearts (Rom. 2:15), and this stirs men to keep raising moral and religious questions and seek a better world. Mankind is restlessly waiting for a just society to be built. Yet men fail to build it because they themselves can only attempt change by law, by revolution, or as Mumford suggests, by dreaming. The rule of men inevitably fails, laws never issue in what is desired, and dreams evaporate.

Renewal and reconciliation come from God alone, by grace, through Christ. Christ alone offers the solid foundation of hope for a transformed world, reconciled people, justice, and peace. The future is God's, and his reconciling purpose will be accomplished. In the end there will be one kingdom, and that will be Christ's. It takes faith to believe that, but once accepted it gives meaning to whatever else is required along the way.

Paul's message is basic to our understanding of and engagement in urban mission. There is a loss of confidence today in the simple message of the gospel. Sincere Christians are being led to believe that sophisticated urbanites need something new, something more glamorous or more relevant to their needs than the doctrine of reconciliation with God through faith in Christ Jesus. "Need" is being defined in a purely humanistic and materialistic manner, and the need for justification and reconciliation with God are left out of the picture. This subtle shift away from the biblical message explains to a large extent why Protestant churches in general have been ineffectual in the city.

Paul knew he had something to say to the cities which he visited. His message came from God, and Paul saw himself as its messenger. Secular and radical theologians today are wrestling with real problems, and they describe their wrestlings passionately and convincingly in many books. Unfortunately, some of them have drawn the conclusion that we really have no divine and authoritative message for urban man. We must identify with him, sit with him in his misery, and let him talk to us. But there is little that we can say to him, and trying to "convert" him to our own religious position is out of place.

The contemporary urban world needs to be studied and understood by those whom God has called to be communicators of his Word. Too often evangelical missionaries have preached to the air because their feet were not on the ground. They did not understand the people to whom they spoke. But it is the tragedy of tragedies to lose one's grasp on the historic, biblical gospel, which is reconciliation with God through conversion to Jesus Christ. Paul never confused contemporary needs with eternal priorities, and neither should we.

Paul Versus Marx on How to Produce the "New Man"

Paul's fundamental meassage to the urban world of the first century has another application to one of the burning questions facing us today. Around the world, Marxism and Christianity are pitted against each other, ideologically and practically. They are based on opposite principles, the one being materialistic and the other theistic. They aim to lead men in opposite directions, the one toward a society ruled by human power and reason and the other toward the kingdom of Jesus Christ. Some Christians believe that Christians and Marxists can cooperate fruitfully in accomplishing certain short-range goals. I would challenge this position, because I believe that any such cooperation between people of opposing loyalties beclouds the fundamental issues that separate them and proves to be a stumbling block to those who do not perceive the underlying differences.

The issue which is a basic dividing line between the message of Paul and the teaching of Karl Marx has to do with how the "new man" is produced. Paul moved about the world of his day—a world filled with injustice, oppression, and corruption of all kinds—preaching a way out of the mire for people and the society they had produced by means of spiritual new birth. "If any man is in Christ," wrote Paul, "he is a new creature. Old things are passed away, and everything is become new" (II Cor. 5:17).

Marxists also talk about new people and the importance of producing them. They recognize that the Marxist's ultimate goal of the ideal society cannot be attained until man himself is changed. Already in 1843, Feuerbach, the famous critic of religion, was writing to Karl Marx, "We need new men!" He realized that the old ones could not be relied upon to bring about brotherhood and create a new society, and that merely to set men free is no guarantee that they would become better. Political emancipation by itself has not brought about brotherhood or put an end to selfishness. Man himself must be changed, and therein lies the problem.

How can the new man be produced? This question lies at the heart of the conflict between Christianity and Marxism. The fundamental antagonism between Christianity and Marxism does not lie in the formal description of the ideal man so much as in the choice of the road that must be taken to produce this new kind of creature. According to Marxist theory, the new man must be produced by man himself, through re-education and the re-ordering of social structures. The Bible, on the other hand, teaches that only God can create new people. Liberation from self-worship or any other form of idolatry is a gift from God, and it is something which God alone can perform.

Communist literature in recent years brings to light some of the frustration felt by communists in regard to the problem of creating the new man. The creation of the new man is recognized as the most difficult task in the communist transformation of society, for without it the communist ideal of a world in which people will perform their duties voluntarily, unselfishly, in perfect harmony with each other, and for the common good, cannot be achieved. It is gradually recognized that political and economic revolutions in themselves cannot produce a situation in which the birth of the unselfish man takes place automatically. Evil, or "the weed" as one writer calls it, cannot be eradicated so easily. The lust to possess, to dominate, and even to destroy for selfish purposes, is part of the human make-up, and revolutionary changes in politics and economics do not make it disappear. Instead of eradicating evil, the totalitarian state upon which the implementation of communism depends tends to grow stronger and more unbearable because its powers and authority are so much greater. It finally produces a soulless bureaucracy, which completely regiments human life and tolerates no opposition.

Paul's approach to how the new man is produced stands in sharp contrast to Marxist theory. Paul was a preacher, not a political or social revolutionary. He believed that the new humanity would be produced by God's grace in men's hearts through the Holy Spirit, and that the verbal proclamation of the gospel was the principal means God chose to use to accomplish this change. In Christianity, transformation takes place first on the *inside*, and then, through obedience to God and the work of the Spirit, brotherhood and reconciliation between individuals and classes are produced. This fundamental presupposition, which is a matter of faith, spells the difference between the Pauline approach to urban renewal and all Marxist-humanist strategies.

At the same time it must be said that the only way Christians can show that the gospel does indeed produce fruits offering hope to a distressed world is by living the kind of life that Paul taught his converts in the first century. In a time when so many are searching desperately for a way out of social and economic morass, heavy responsibility rests upon Christians to adorn their message with the credible witness of their lives. Until the texture of our lives bears the stamp of Christ's righteousness, the world will not believe that Christians really make a difference.

Chapter 6

Paul

The Urban Strategist—His Method

On a warm night in July, 1977, the lights suddenly went out in five boroughs of New York City. Within seconds the sounds of bricks and stones could be heard smashing store windows as looters ravaged stores, fought one another for choice pieces of merchandise, and hauled home as much as they could steal and carry away.

The behavior of New York's looters shocked the nation. For it was not, as some commentators first tried to make out, that these people were hungry and needed food to live. Most of the looters had full-time jobs. Of the 145 Brooklyn stores which they looted, only 12 were supermarkets, grocery stores, or butcher shops. The rest included 39 furniture stores, 21 appliance stores, 20 pharmacies, 17 jewelry stores, 10 clothing stores, 8 shoe stores, 7 liquor stores, 7 department or variety stores, and 4 auto supply stores. These were not hungry people craving for food, but ordinary inhabitants of the nation's largest city suddenly given the chance to take what was not theirs, to break down and destroy the property of others, and to get away with it under the cover of city-wide darkness.

One columnist, Ella Mary Sims, had this to say about the looting:

> The whole picture of thousands of people stealing— and so quickly after the lights were out—speaks of an attitude of violence that is never far beneath the surface of our lives. We may not think of stealing, looting and burning as being violent, but in New York if the

pressure had been applied by store owners or mer-
chants, some of those who were stealing could very
well be murderers today.
> *The sickness of New York in the dark is a gripping fact of
> life throughout the world. As of now, none of us knows the
> cause or the cure.*[1]

No sensible person would minimize the complexity of urban
problems or pretend that one simple solution, even a profoundly
religious one, would make all the problems disappear overnight.
The "sickness of New York," to use Ella Mary Sims's expression,
is terrifying, and not least of all because it is essentially the same
throughout the world. But where we disagree with Ms. Sims is
with her conclusion that "none of us knows the cause or the
cure." The Bible tells us what the cause is and where the cure
must be found. The cause, as Jonah informed Nineveh, lies in the
sinfulness of the people, and the cure is through Jesus Christ as
revealed in the gospel. At this crucial point in their analysis of the
city and its problems, Christians part company with secularists.

How does the person who senses God's call to minister in
Christ's name to city people formulate his approach? What kind
of missionary strategy has any hope of success against such
odds? The city contains so many wrongs which need to be recti-
fied and so many people without Christ that the first temptation
is to give up in despair because the job is too big. The second
temptation, equally dangerous, is to forget the essentials, con-
fuse priorities, and lavish all one's resources on commendable
activities that are not of primary importance.

Scripture does not bind us to one particular missionary
methodology, for the New Testament itself reveals a variety of
approaches and emphases. Moreover, there are available to us
today a vast variety of evangelistic media, products of modern
technology of which the early apostles never dreamed but which
God in his providence has provided and expects us to use to the
best of our ability to spread the gospel.

But are there not certain basic elements in apostolic missionary
strategy which are transcendent and might help us in our approach to today's cities? I am convinced that there are. Paul's
strategy in the cities of the Roman Empire can and should guide

---

[1] *The Grand Rapids Press*, 30 July 1977, italics mine.

us today, for his strategy rested on biblical teachings that are as authoritative and practical today as they were then.

The Conversion of Sinners

The lines of Paul's urban strategy ran from converts, to churches, to the whole Roman society—its governments, institutions, and religions. Paul moved out into the highly urbanized Roman world of his day with a definite strategy in mind. He had confidence regarding the essentials of his message and method. Some doors might remain closed and frustrations and rejection might come, but Paul knew what a missionary was supposed to do. He had a strategy based on biblical presuppositions concerning man's sin and God's salvation.

Paul's missionary strategy was built on the bedrock of personal repentance and conversion. His own experience of conversion served to remind him of the absolute necessity for radical spiritual change. In his earlier life Paul had had religion, morality, zeal, and social status (Phil. 3:4-6). But none of these, nor all of them combined, had been able to give him peace with God. He needed to be converted to Christ at a definite time and place, and until that occurred nothing really mattered (cf. Phil. 3:7-9).

To Paul, being "in" or "outside" of Christ was an absolute and all-important difference. That truth must be emphasized because religious universalism blurs the basic distinction. It was not any easier for Paul than it is for us to insist that Christianity demands a clear-cut break with all other religious commitments and a radical moral change in the lives of its adherents. The spirit of Hellenism did not favor such absolutizing of one religion over another. Hellenistic man had a convenient way of separating what a person believed from the way he worshiped and personal ethics from whatever a person might think about God. But Paul came preaching the necessity of conversion and total commitment to the Lord Jesus. He insisted that the sovereign God of the Scriptures required an entire realignment of heart and action.

The first touchstone of an authentic urban strategy is: Are people confronted with the saviorhood and lordship of Christ and urged to surrender their hearts and lives to him? Urban evangelism has had more than its share of easy "decisionism," and it has left the city unchanged and unimpressed. The exigencies of city life allow neither a wishy-washy presentation of the Christian faith and life nor a sidestepping of the necessity of personal conversion. Cities need renewal, and on this we all agree. But let nobody be so foolish as to think that we can begin anywhere else than where Paul began, with radically changed people, converted in their hearts to serving God in the midst of the city.

The Establishment of Churches

The second key element in Paul's urban strategy was the establishment of churches. Paul was never satisfied with simply bringing individuals to Christ. He organized churches wherever he could, and the incorporation of believers into permanent Christian communities was basic to his entire approach to the city.

Obviously Paul maintained a very high view of the church and its divinely instituted structure, and he was committed to its growth and expansion. Formerly he had been a persecutor of the church, but Christ Jesus himself had stopped all that when he revealed himself on the road to Damascus and said, "I am Jesus whom you are persecuting." That experience settled a number of things for Paul. He knew from that moment on who Jesus was, and what the church was. The church in some mysterious way was nothing less than the body of Christ, and what was done to the church was done to Christ.

Within a few days of his conversion Paul was actively advancing the gospel and promoting the local Christian community at Damascus. By revelation he had come to understand that the church was the long-awaited messianic community, the bearer of the gospel to all races and nations. It was through the church that God would now fulfill his redemptive purpose for the world.

That insight made Paul a church planter. Since God in Christ was carrying out his long-awaited redemptive work in the world through the instrumentality of the church, Paul knew that the expansion of the church was a matter of highest priority. Evangelism therefore meant proclaiming the gospel and gathering believers into visible, organized congregations. If he could not stay long enough to complete the work of appointing elders himself, he delegated the responsibility to one of his coworkers (cf. Titus 1:5). For Paul, the work was not completed until a visible, organized church was established as an abiding witness to the city.

Paul's church-planting strategy differs considerably from much of what goes by the name of urban mission in our time. In conservative circles, urban mission generally does not go much beyond the skid-row rescue mission strategy or the city-wide evangelistic campaign. Sometimes the mass media, such as radio and television, are substituted for person-to-person contact. In more liberal churches, urban mission has come to mean heavy involvement in race relations, efforts to improve lower-class housing, and social services of various kinds. These in themselves may be legitimate forms of Christian service, and their testimony may at times lead people to inquire about Christ and the love that motivates such service. But if these activities stand alone, they are incomplete. The gospel needs to be verbalized as well as actualized, and the will of God that believers be brought together into living cells of the body of Christ called churches must not be left out of urban mission.

On numerous occasions in the New Testament we find mention made of "the church in your house" (Rom. 16:5; I Cor. 16:19; Col. 4:15, and similar references). We know that for two centuries Christians did not erect special edifices in which to worship God but used private homes, rented quarters, or whatever might be available for their gatherings. In Rome as well as in other cities of the Empire, groups of believers met in scattered places throughout the city. When Paul said to the Ephesian elders that he had taught them the whole counsel of God "publicly and from house to house," he was probably referring to his visits not simply to individual families but to the homes where groups of believers gathered regularly for worship and instruction. Today we often call these gatherings "house churches." There are thousands of such groups in Third World cities, and they are a growing phenomenon in Western cities as well. In one city in the Netherlands, where declining attendance at Protestant churches prompted a city-wide religious survey, it was discovered that more than 300 weekly gatherings were being held in private homes and rented quarters. Sometimes the venue is in an apartment building, or a store-front. It may even be in the open air on a vacant lot, as happens occasionally in poor barrios of Third World cities. But regardless of where it is held, the meeting consists of Christians and inquirers gathering to hear God's Word, sing his praise, build up one another, and witness to the unsaved.

Cell groups and neighborhood churches have a far greater potential for evangelistic growth than do the big downtown churches upon which some people try to depend for urban penetration. Instead of concentrating on big cathedral-like churches which try to serve the city from a few central locations, today's situation calls for a return to the multi-locational strategy of the early Christians. On this subject Paulus Scharpff has written:

> "The one and only way to genuine fellowship is the creation of truly Christian cell-groups in the midst of the aridity of modern life; it is the indirect way to mutual reconstruction, to united witness, and outside service" (H. Kraemer).
>
> An evangelistic cell-group is a fellowship of pastoral care in which members first minister spiritually to one another before they unite in an outside witness. . . .
>
> Evangelistic cell-groups are a special means for cultivating the gifts of grace, for they are the best spiritual organisms available to the church of Jesus Christ. They are necessary so long as we are people of flesh and blood, and so long as the law of nature obtains that all organic life grows from small cells.[2]

Witnessing to Christ's Lordship in Society and the World

Paul's strategy for mission moved from converts to churches, from churches to the city as a whole, and from there to the entire known world. He intended that the leaven of the gospel be felt everywhere. In *The City of God*, Augustine beautifully depicts this process:

> After the community or City comes the whole earth, wherein is placed the third stage of human society, which begins from the household, then extends to the city, and finally to the world (XIX, 7).

Jesus Christ is the ascended Lord, and that lordship means sovereignty over nations and their leaders and the world in all its

But now in fundamentally chp?

---

[2] Paulus Scharpff, *History of Evangelism* (Grand Rapids: William B. Eerdmans Publishing Co., 1964), pp. 339, 341.

complexity, as well as over the redemptive community of the church. For the nations are now the exalted Son's inheritance and the uttermost parts of the earth his rightful possession (Ps. 2:8).

There is a breadth in Paul's perspective that has often gone unnoticed in evangelical circles, and this probably explains the narrow and individualistic approach of many traditional missionary strategies. The people whom Paul led to Christ and the churches that he organized were intended to be a leaven in society, models of righteousness, and signs of Christ's kingdom. *but not all beh/ordinary* His insistence that church leaders be men of exemplary behavior and the attention he paid to disciplinary matters were motivated from two sides. Internally, Paul was concerned that the church be pure and unspotted by the world, like a virgin bride awaiting her husband. Externally, the church was a sign to the world of God's transforming grace, a living symbol of Christ's kingdom and his lordship among men. For Paul, Christ's lordship was here-and-now as well as future. It affected the Christian's whole approach to life and the world. No area was to be excluded. New life in Christ meant living under God's sovereignty, according to his Word, as sons and daughters of the King. In Paul's strategy, the leaven of the kingdom entered society through the changed lives of converted people and the churches which they composed.

The early Christians have been rightly called the "reforming party" of the Roman Empire.[3] They came mainly from the lower classes and knew from experience the bitterness of poverty, slavery, and all the oppressive factors inherent in Roman society. They did not call for violence or the radical overthrow of government. But they did bring about change, often paying with their own blood the price for their convictions. They did this because Paul and the other apostles had laid the basic foundation of the church in the Word of God, which everywhere and always challenges evil, oppression, and injustice.

It is instructive to note that Friedrich Engels, collaborator with Karl Marx on the *Communist Manifesto* and chief propagandist for Marx's ideas through the editing and publication of Marx's writings, devoted considerable attention to the origins and development of the Christian religion and took special note of the social

---

[3] William M. Ramsay, *The Cities of St. Paul: Their Influence on His Life and Thought* (1907; reprint ed., Grand Rapids: Baker Book House, 1960), pp. 72-75.

consciousness of early Christians. Engels drew four parallels between the early Christian movement and the modern working-class movement: both originated among poor and oppressed [1] people; both proclaimed a message of salvation from bondage [2] and hope for the oppressed; both were persecuted, discriminated [3] against, and despised by the powerful and privileged; and both [4] forged irresistibly ahead despite all these difficulties.[4]

Most of us will reject Engels's way of interpreting history in terms of the class struggle, and we consider his assessment of what actually occurred in the first century as sadly deficient respecting the most important element of all, namely, the vertical dimension of the power and providence of God. Engels chose to see only the socio-economic factors and interpreted the historical events exclusively in terms of the struggle between the privileged and the oppressed. Absent from his analysis is what Luke referred to in his description of the growth of the Christian movement: "And day by day the Lord added to their number those whom he was saving" (Acts 2:47). But having said this, it must also be added that Engels, better than many modern evangelical Christians, recognized the socially revolutionary character of early Christianity. As the early Christians were instructed by the Word of God, they became increasingly aware of the basic issues at stake and the intrinsic differences between their faith in God and the false idolatries of the Roman Empire. Full perception of the deep spiritual issues involved did not occur overnight, nor did the answers come at once. But gradually the false gods of Rome were identified, the battle joined, and the idols began to fall. Faith in action, rather than the barren economic determinism by which Marx and Engels explain history, prompted the conflicts and the changes that occurred.

People who possess a vision of the lordship of Christ and the kingdom which he established constitute the hope of modern cities. For that reason it is so important that from cathedral pulpits to humble shanty churches the full gospel of Christ the Savior and Lord be announced. *The degree of a convert's transformation and the impact on society which a church can make are in direct*

---

[4] *Marx and Engels on Religion* (Moscow: Foreign Language Publishing House, 1957), pp. 313-43. Cited in José Miguez Bonino, *Doing Theology in a Revolutionary Situation* (Philadelphia: Fortress Press, 1975), p. 132.

proportion to the breadth of the gospel they hear. If city pulpits would universally proclaim the comprehensive biblical message of Christ crucified, risen, exalted, and reigning, people would be converted in greater number and urban society would feel the impact. Bible-directed Christians perceive the issues, know where the battle lines should be drawn, and understand the demonic nature of urban idolatry. They realize that the gospel is intended to be more than a personal and private affair. It is also meant for the marketplace, the chambers of government, the schools, and the courts of the land. Millions are seeking that kind of faith, and it is the duty of the church to proclaim it verbally and concretely. *All failed for 1900 years?*

Paul's Method at Ephesus

The New Testament provides a detailed account of Paul's strategy for the evangelization of the city of Ephesus and its surrounding area. Books on missions commonly refer to various facets of Paul's work in this city, but I have never seen his entire involvement at Ephesus viewed in a broad and comprehensive way as a model for urban evangelism. That is how I would like to look at it now.

Five stages are evident in Paul's approach to Ephesus. His initial contact with the city is recorded in Acts 18 (RSV). Paul had just completed more than a year and a half of "teaching the word of God" in the city of Corinth (v. 11), and he was hastening to get back to Antioch of Syria with the report of his second missionary journey. He was accompanied up to this point by his friends and converts, Priscilla and Aquila.

Paul's method at Ephesus was to make a contact at the local synagogue and plant the seed of the gospel among the local Jews. Some seemed receptive and urged him to stay longer. But Paul did not have time just then, and he could only promise that he would return "if God wills" (v. 21).

Initial contacts of a similar nature are available in abundance in many parts of today's world. Evangelical radio and television programs, literature, correspondence courses, Bible distribution, and mass evangelism campaigns have laid the groundwork and now await the follow-up. There is no shortage of initial contacts. What is needed is a better missionary strategy for following through on these contacts to lead inquirers to become disciples and to establish churches among them.

The second stage in the Ephesus strategy did not involve Paul directly. It involved Priscilla and Aquila, whom Paul had left at Ephesus (v. 19), possibly for the purpose of establishing a Christian beachhead in that city. A powerful preacher named Apollos came to Ephesus and began to announce the gospel of Jesus Christ in the Jewish synagogue. Luke's account indicates that Apollos was not only eloquent as a speaker and fervent in the presentation of his message, but he was well-versed in the Bible and dared to refute the Jews publicly, "proving from the Scriptures that Jesus was the Christ" (vv. 24-28). But Apollos also had certain shortcomings. When Paul's friends, Priscilla and Aquila, heard Apollos speak, they realized that his doctrinal understanding needed some straightening out. Without doubt he preached Jesus Christ, but his knowledge was incomplete and he needed further instruction. The lay couple, Priscilla and Aquila, took care of this, with the result that Apollos's zeal and fervency were then balanced by doctrinal knowledge, and his ministry was accordingly enriched.

Apollos did not stay long in Ephesus. He soon expressed the desire to cross the sea westward to continue his ministry in Achaia. By then there was a nucleus of believers in Ephesus, for Luke wrote that "the brethren encouraged him" and wrote the disciples in Achaia (probably in the city of Corinth) that they should welcome him (v. 27). When Apollos arrived, he repeated the kind of sincere and earnest ministry that he had had in Ephesus, with the result that the Corinthian Christians also were strengthened in the faith (vv. 27, 28).

One of the significant characteristics of today's world is that everywhere in Asia, Africa, Latin America, and also in North America, God is raising up thousands of homespun indigenous leaders like Apollos. They are men and women who are zealous about personal witnessing. They are fervent in preaching, and unfortunately, they are often inaccurate on a number of points of doctrine. Such people are not known for their prolonged ministry in any one place, which is good since they lack the qualifications for in-depth teaching and organization. But regardless of their weaknesses, they are key people as far as the spread of the gospel is concerned. Their zeal for evangelism is unrivaled among "organization" people. They demonstrate great courage in carrying the gospel into difficult areas and are not ashamed to speak out for Christ when all they can expect is opposition, scorn, and mistreatment.

These are the "evangelists" about whom Paul wrote in Ephesians 4:11 describing them as being among Christ's precious gifts to his church. Evangelists have a special endowment from the Lord that enables them to explain the gospel in clear and effective ways to unsaved people. When they preach or testify, Jesus Christ is lifted up winsomely and powerfully, and the Holy Spirit performs the miracle of new birth and conversion. When evangelists like Apollos are not around, churches grow very slowly. But when they are present, things happen! They may require certain "straightening out" at times, because precision of expression, doctrinal details, and organizational procedures are not their strong points. But only those people who are blind to evangelism will minimize the importance of evangelists. They are key instruments in God's hands for the spread of the gospel and the building of the church. At Ephesus, Apollos was an important link between Paul's initial contact and his deeper and prolonged ministry later on.

The third stage in Paul's involvement at Ephesus is described in Acts 19. It was a ministry which he shared with Timothy, his assistant. Paul's goal upon his return to Ephesus was to evangelize in such a way that a church could be organized. Through that nucleus of believers the city and the region beyond it would be penetrated by the gospel. Paul did not have to wait very long before seeing this goal accomplished. Acts 19:9-10 tells us: " . . . He [Paul] took the disciples with him and had discussions daily. . . . This went on for two years, so that all the Jews and Greeks who lived in the province of Asia heard the word of the Lord" (NIV).

The steps Paul took in pursuit of this goal included first of all correcting the faith and expanding the spiritual knowledge of the disciples who were already there. Paul found that he had to introduce them to the person and work of the Holy Spirit, about whom they had not been instructed. The result was that the "Ephesian Pentecost" occurred and the believers "spoke in tongues and prophesied" (Acts 19:6). The circle of believers at that time consisted of about twelve men in all (Acts 19:7).

The synagogue, comprised of Jews and Gentile proselytes (as the synagogues of the Dispersion generally were), was the natural religious bridge into the city, and Paul made full use of it. In the synagogue were people who knew the Old Testament and its prophecies concerning the Messiah and the New Age that he would usher in. Many of them were bilingual and bicultural. They had contacts in key places throughout the city and empire. Though eventually it became necessary for Paul to withdraw from the synagogue because of the opposition of the gospel rejectors, he used this contact for as long as the door remained open. When Paul left the synagogue he took the disciples with him and transferred his center of operation to the lecture hall of Tyrannus. This place then became his "pulpit" to the city, and daily for two years he carried on discussions with a view to leading men to discipleship.

During this time signs and miracles began to accompany Paul's ministry. Ephesus was a center of occult worship and practice. Demonic powers were not merely the result of superstitious fear; they were real and exercised a terrible control over men's lives. Those powers were now challenged by a name more powerful than any Ephesus had ever heard before: the name of the Lord Jesus, by which evil spirits were cast out and populations made to tremble (Acts 19:13, 17). By signs and miracles, the divine origin of Paul's ministry was authenticated. There is no evidence that miracles of this kind were a continuing mark of the church's life or even of Timothy's ministry at a later date. But unquestionably, the extraordinary signs that accompanied Paul's work at Ephesus added tremendous impetus to the spread of the gospel.

Paul's residency was cut short by a riot, and Timothy was later required to complete what Paul had begun. Paul could look back on his work at Ephesus, as he did in his farewell speech recorded in Acts 20, and say that in his heart he felt that he was innocent of the blood of all men, for he had performed his ministry faithfully, declaring to them publicly and from house to house all that they needed to know: the whole counsel of God and the gospel of the kingdom. Through his ministry Paul had trained local leaders into whose hands he could entrust the care of the flock. These were appointed as "overseers" and "shepherds of the church of God" (Acts 20:28, NIV). Their appointment was from the Holy Spirit, witnessed to by the laying on of hands (Acts

20:28; I Tim. 5:22). Their training came through Paul's ministry and that of Timothy, which followed.

What Paul found at Ephesus is not uncommon in many places today. In our ministry in Latin America, for example, we regularly receive appeals from small, young congregations that have sprung up through mass evangelism and the work of untrained, independent evangelists. In visiting these groups we find that there is often confusion concerning the person and work of the Holy Spirit. Occultism is also a problem, for most of the believers come from backgrounds filled with superstition, and spiritism is practiced all around them. The goddess of Ephesus was named Diana, and Latin America has virtually made a goddess of the Virgin Mary. There was violence against the young church in Ephesus, and there are places today where Christians are experiencing subtle forms of oppression (and some that are not so subtle) because they acknowledge the Lord Jesus.

What is needed is a mobile missionary ministry that would send men and women to serve as instructors and organizers of such groups so that they could come to know and believe the true faith and form viable churches. Missionary residency in most cases would not be longer than two to four years. Emphasis would fall on teaching the Word of God, correcting errors, and training responsible disciples so that the church could carry on after the missionary has left.

The following quotation from a letter written by Arnold Rumph, a Christian Reformed missionary to Puerto Rico, illustrates how this method might be applied to a concrete situation. In this letter, Rumph reports a trip that he had made to the neighboring nation of the Dominican Republic after he had learned that a group of believers was in the process of organizing what they called a "Christian Reformed Church."

> A few weeks ago I visited a group of believers in the Dominican Republic. I came in contact with them by means of the follow-up correspondence of *La Hora de la Reforma* (our denominational broadcast, *The Back to God Hour*). It's a group that has some Pentecostal leanings but no relationship with any existing denomination.
>
> The people are extremely poor. The pastor and the men of the congregation with whom I spent several hours told me that they were very impressed by the radio broadcast and wanted to identify their church

with the denomination which sponsored the broadcast. So, on the Sunday before my arrival, they put up a signboard in front of their humble church building: *"La Iglesia Cristiana Reformada."*

My first visit with this church was an unforgettable experience. The Sunday morning service began at 9:30 and lasted until 12:15 p.m. A total of twenty-one people were present. There were two children, six women and thirteen men. At their request I preached and explained to them the basic doctrines of the Christian Church. They know and believe the essentials, without a doubt. But there is an awful lot that still needs to be taught, and some things must be corrected.

I was particularly impressed by the fact that there were so many men in the service in comparison to the number of women and children. It appears that the group has about fifty-five members and sympathizers, but on that particular day many could not attend because they had to work in the sugar cane.

What do they want from us? Basically, teaching. They have a pastor, but he never had any training and can hardly read. He's a man of two books, his Bible and his hymnbook. I preached for an hour and they begged for more. That shows how hungry they are for instruction. There are a number of reasons why this group has stuck together and not drifted off to some other denomination. Most of them owe their religious experience to the pastor who was the first to be converted and began witnessing to his family and co-workers in the sugar cane. They follow him as their leader but they know they need instruction beyond what he can give.

I taught them what I could on this first visit and promised to send them biblical material which they could use in their weekly Bible classes. I promised them too that I would ask our Board to allow us to visit them a couple of times a year for intensive periods of instruction. I think that with a flexible set-up which combines regular letters of advice and encouragement, printed Bible study materials, and periodic visits from Puerto Rico we can see this church make real progress. There are a number of other opportunities like this waiting for us in the Caribbean, and I hope we can follow through with them.

This missionary had the right idea, and the strategy he proposed has been adopted and is working well. The media explosion in evangelism has planted seeds of faith in many places, but unless mobile missionaries follow up on these contacts most of the seedlings will be lost to the cultists and other of the devil's agents. Needed are modern "Pauls" who know the language of the area, have had experience in cross-cultural evangelism, possess the gift of teaching, and are allowed the degree of mobility which will allow them to move in when opportunities are presented. They must also know Christian doctrine and how to teach and apply it to fresh needs and new situations. Finally, they must understand the basics of church polity so that they can train believers in Christian discipleship and responsible local leadership.

The fourth stage in the Ephesus plan for urban evangelization consists of periodic follow-up visits. The Book of Acts states plainly that follow-up was one of the secrets of Paul's strategy, and "the Pastoral Epistles imply a number of journeys which cannot be fitted into the itineraries of Paul that are recorded in the book of Acts."[5] Paul returned to the places where he had established beachheads for the gospel to nourish and encourage the new believers. He also sent his assistants, men like Timothy, Titus, and Tychicus (I Tim. 1:3; Titus 1:5; and Eph. 6:21, 22), to convey messages, correct false teachings, organize churches, and pastor believers.

Today, mission leaders are aware that we are moving rapidly away from the stage of missions in which Western missionaries "dug in" at one place and remained there for many years. Hardly anywhere in the world can a missionary say for sure that he will not be forced out either by the government or various nationalist influences. At the same time, more contracts and opportunities are open to missionaries than ever before. Travel is fast and relatively easy, and never has follow-up been easier than it is now. At a time when foreign domination of national churches is deeply resented and every semblance of paternalism needs to be avoided, it seems that Paul's Ephesus plan has a great deal to offer by way of guidance toward an effective increase of urban churches without dependence on long-term missionary residence or control.

---

[5] William Hendriksen, *Bible Survey* (Grand Rapids: Baker Book House, 1961), p. 419.

Even as I say this, however, I want to clarify a related point about which I feel very deeply. It concerns the missionary's identification with and relationship to the Christians in the young church that the missionary hopes to build up. The intimacy of Paul's contacts with churches like that of Ephesus is very striking. His stay in their midst was not an extensive one, but while he was there he lived very intensively with those who responded to his preaching. His letters indicate how extensive, intimate, and personal was their knowledge of him, and his of them. Paul understood his mission as that of nurturing men to Christian maturity, and this required establishing close personal relationships with them. He knew that he could not deepen their faith and lead them to follow his example if he at the same time kept them "at arm's length." In this connection it is worth pondering a statement which Willis P. De Boer makes in his book *The Imitation of Paul.*

> The church of today has resources available in its work of evangelism and Christian nurture of which Paul could not have dreamed. There is now great opportunity of multiplying one man's voice through public address systems, microphones, television cameras, printing presses, duplicating machines, addressographs. There is much emphasis in Christianity on doing things in a big way and in reaching and serving large numbers of people. The influence of close personal relationships, of example and of imitation does not lend itself to these easy processes of multiplication. Are close personal relationships, imitation, and example to be regarded as obsolete for present-day Christianity? Is it possible that they are too time-consuming for such critical times as these? One finds difficulty projecting Paul into the present situation. However, it is noteworthy that Paul's time-consuming personal working and living with people did bring forth results which were neither trivial nor insignificant. Perhaps the church of Christ would be well-served with more Christian leaders working at a slower pace, limiting their contacts and activities, and opening their personal Christian lives sufficiently to permit of imitation—be it only by a few.[6]

---

[6] Willis Peter De Boer, *The Imitation of Paul: An Exegetical Study* (Kampen, the Netherlands: J. H. Kok, 1962), p. 216.

The fifth and final stage of Paul's ministry to Ephesus is represented by his Epistle to the Ephesian church. I consider this letter to be a kind of six-chapter "extension course" in doctrine, ethics, and practical Christian piety. The letter was probably intended for a wide circle of house churches and growing congregations. Written during Paul's first Roman imprisonment, the epistle provided solid nourishment for the growth toward maturity of the Christians to whom it was sent.

When should a missionary leave? When should control be turned over to the national church? These are important questions which every missionary and mission organization faces. Sometimes the apostle Paul was not faced with the question because he had to run for his life and leave the young churches earlier than he intended. But one of the strikingly beautiful features of Paul's farewell to the elders of Ephesus was his deep trust in the power of the Word and the Spirit to nourish and protect them in the days ahead. This ought to be the goal of every missionary, the planting of a church like that at Ephesus, to whose leaders it can be said without a doubt or delay: "And now I commend you to God and to the word of his grace, which is able to build you up and to give you the inheritance among all those who are sanctified" (Acts 20:32, RSV).

Postscript to Answer an Objection

Trusting the Word and Spirit is difficult for us to do. We tend to believe that our presence and control are indispensable and the young churches cannot survive without us. In this vein, and I hope that I am not misjudging them, some mission leaders have objected to Paul's approach, calling it superficial as a general policy and admissible only in emergency situations. This forces us to consider how effective Paul's strategy really was. Three decades later, what remained of the churches he had established? We cannot blame his strategy for the destruction wrought by the hordes of Moslems several centuries later, but we do have a right to inquire as to the endurance of a church like Ephesus within a reasonable period and on the basis of the information we have available.

When Paul, during his first Roman imprisonment, wrote the Epistle to the Ephesians, he did not so much as hint that things were going wrong in the church. Five years had passed since

Paul's stay in the city, but no discouraging news had reached the apostle's ears. Instead, Paul gave thanks to God for their love to all the saints (Eph. 1:15) and without any reservation drew them into the deep and mysterious relationship between human love and divine (Eph. 5:22-33).

The last word about Ephesus came from Christ himself (Rev. 2:1-7). Ephesus was the first of the seven churches to be addressed by the exalted Lord through revelation to the apostle John. The Ephesian church was by that time in serious danger, for its members had forsaken their first love (Rev. 2:4). The outward structures and formal adherences were still present, but the inner devotion to Christ and the spiritual power that had once been there were almost gone.

What had gone wrong? Had Paul's strategy proven to be weak? Was he mistaken in trusting the pastoral care of this flock to the spiritual overseeing of the elders? Not at all. What had happened at Ephesus was that a new generation of members had grown up during the thirty-plus years since the church was established, and while they were heirs of the traditions they had lost much of the power. The forms that for their parents had been filled with life still survived, but the life had departed. They preserved the outlines of Christian truth, but their love for him who is the Truth had grown cold. That is why Christ called them to repentance.

This needs to be remembered whenever we hear arguments to the effect that Paul's strategy in Acts was generally circumstantial and justifiable only in emergencies. The churches which Paul established did not last forever, but the things that went wrong at places like Ephesus were not due to inherent faults in his strategy. Actually, the first generation of Ephesian Christians kept the faith very well and attained unparalleled heights of spiritual maturity. We note the "heights" from which Christ reminds them they had fallen (Rev. 2:5). But thirty years later another generation had arisen and the glory was departed. That could happen regardless of the length of time the founding missionary might have remained. What Christ's Word to the Ephesian church clearly implied was this: each successive generation of Christians must embrace Christ by faith personally and appropriate for themselves the apostles' teachings and example, or otherwise they will fall like Ephesus and lose the great heritage they received.